ORIGIN AND EVOLUTION
OF DOUBLE ENTRY BOOKKEEPING

Origin and Evolution of Double Entry Bookkeeping

A STUDY

OF ITALIAN PRACTICE

FROM THE FOURTEENTH CENTURY

By Edward Peragallo, Ph. D.

WITH A FOREWORD BY ROBERT H. MONTGOMERY

NEW YORK

AMERICAN INSTITUTE PUBLISHING COMPANY

1938

TO MY MOTHER

FOREWORD

T HE *principal value of the study which Mr. Peragallo has made is that it establishes beyond dispute two things: first, that by its very nature accounting adapts itself to business procedure, not business to accounting procedure; and, second, that for centuries after the first signs of double entry appeared, accountants and teachers and writers of accounting were concerned, not with theory, but exclusively with business transactions and their description in the accounts. Accounting theory first appeared in the nineteenth century, and there followed an epidemic of so-called systems of bookkeeping — most of them fantastic and utterly useless for practical purposes.*

To the practitioner who looks upon his work as the systematic application of knowledge and skill in effecting a desired result, it is clear that to attribute to his methods the inviolability of natural laws would hinder rather than help him in his search for truth and stunt the growth of an art already hard pressed to adapt itself to the increasing demands of business. There is reason to fear that some in authority have such a misunderstanding of the nature of accounting; this is the only conclusion which can be drawn from their tendency to expect business to conform to an accounting pattern rather than the reverse.

At its present stage of development, accounting, although still far from perfect, serves remarkably well the purpose for which it has always been intended. Accounting is the language of finance — a universal language. It is concerned not with the eternal verities, but with the data immediately before it. These data are not precisely measurable with the rule, the scales, or any instrument yet devised by man. They can be measured only to the extent that human nature can be measured, for the value of every item in financial accounts is contingent upon a varying and illusive human factor. Accounting statements and reports are necessarily expressions of opinion, and no better than the ability and judgment of the accountants who prepare them.

Accounting methods which have endured are those which have met the test of the pragmatists — how well do they serve the given purpose? Accounting has but one purpose, to set forth the results of business operations accurately and truthfully. It draws upon the resources of many sciences, but remains an art, varying in effectiveness with the knowledge and skill of the practitioner — this is the lesson of history.

Robert H. Montgomery

Preface

THE vastness of the subject has made it necessary for me to limit my study of the origin and subsequent development of double-entry bookkeeping to events occurring in Italy, where the system originated some time during the thirteenth or fourteenth centuries. The art of bookkeeping was confined to Italy until the sixteenth century, and then, following in the wake of trade, it spread throughout Europe. The parts of this book, therefore, dealing with the period when bookkeeping was exclusively an Italian art, view the field as a whole, while those parts which deal with subsequent years are a partial treatment. It should be borne in mind, however, that the Italian system of double entry to a large extent determined practice in the rest of Europe; it was not until the eighteenth century that Italy experienced any serious rivalry in the field, and ultimately it was double entry, as developed in Italy, that endured.

The book has been arranged so that examples in a foreign language, set in italic type, are followed immediately by a translation in roman type. Notes to which references appear in the text are placed at the end of each chapter.

I am deeply indebted to Professor Roy B. Kester and Professor Archibald H. Stockder for their generous advice, readings of the manuscript, and valuable criticisms; also to Professor Henry Rand Hatfield, Professor Thomas W. Byrnes, and Professor Lynn Thorndike for their reading and helpful criticisms of the manuscript; and to Walter Hausdofer, the librarian of the School of Business at Columbia University, for invaluable aid in locating and selecting source material. To Charles M. Smith, associate editor of the American Institute Publishing Company, I am deeply obligated for his painstaking efforts in organizing the book and improving the style. To Colonel Robert H. Montgomery I am especially grateful for his interest in my work and for the extensive use I made of the collection of ancient accounting manuscripts which he donated to the Business School Library at Columbia University.

Edward Peragallo

CONTENTS

Part I
THE ORIGIN OF DOUBLE ENTRY

Part II
THE LITERATURE OF ACCOUNTING
The First Cycle (1458–1558)

The Second Cycle (1559–1795)

The Third Cycle (1796 To Date)

THE EMERGENCE OF ACCOUNTING THEORY

THEORIES OF DOUBLE ENTRY

METHODS OF DOUBLE ENTRY

Part III

THE FUNCTIONAL DEVELOPMENT OF DOUBLE ENTRY

PART I

THE ORIGIN OF DOUBLE ENTRY

INTRODUCTION

GENOA

FLORENCE

VENICE

FLORENTINE INDUSTRIAL ACCOUNTING

Part I

THE ORIGIN OF DOUBLE ENTRY

INTRODUCTION

BECAUSE of the paucity of recorded facts, there are many theories but very little certainty as to the origin of double-entry bookkeeping. Students of the subject, in an endeavor to give due credit for the invention of the system, offer a wide range of possibilities. Some are inclined to give full credit to one man — Paciolo, who perhaps more frequently than any other has been named as the author of double entry, but the weight of evidence now seems to be against this theory. Others have attempted to trace the origin of double entry to ancient Rome and Greece. Recent students, however, believe that the system originated in Italy during the thirteenth and fourteenth centuries, and are concentrating their efforts upon determining the exact locality of its origin.

It should be borne in mind that systems of bookkeeping come into being because of the necessity of recording transactions arising out of commerce, industry, and government. Bookkeeping is, therefore, dependent on these transactions for its existence, and any changes it undergoes are probably best explained in the light of the changes that occur in business methods. Because of this, double-entry bookkeeping may ultimately be found to have had a relatively independent origin in many localities and to have been first applied to various types of business activities at almost the same time.

It is the purpose of this work to study some of the changes in the procedure of Italian record keeping that led progressively to the origin of the double-entry system and determined the course of its subsequent evolution.

Medieval bookkeeping developed from humble beginnings. At first business transactions, along with other social or political events, were entered in what might be described as a diary, but with the rise of commerce this crude method of record keeping had to give way to a more efficient system. The first double-entry book to appear was the ledger. It had the accounts divided bilaterally or vertically, and was supported by numerous memorandum books. The ledger probably developed from the debtor and creditor relationships of merchants. It is possible that, with the revival of Medieval commerce and with the increasing importance of

1

fairs, the necessities of business exchange forced merchants to keep records comparable to receivable and payable ledgers. Gradually, with the increasing needs of a growing trade, the ledger was made to include assets, liabilities, expenses, and income. The journal appeared considerably later than the ledger. Its purpose was to record in one place the transactions as entered in various memorandum books. The journal entries were arranged in chronological order, and formally classified into debits and credits with full explanations. From the start the journal was the posting medium for the ledger. Double entry was the result of a long culmination of difficulties resulting from the increasing complexities of trade. It came about gradually, almost imperceptibly.

Its origin, therefore, cannot be traced to any one person or group of persons, but belongs rather to the era of the commercial Renaissance and must have been a phenomenon common to the Italian cities which experienced the burst of economic activity of this era.

Chapter I

GENOA

THE Genoese system of bookkeeping probably was a development of the ancient Roman, which shall therefore be described briefly. From what little we know of it, the Roman system was a complicated one. The various books of account used may conveniently be divided into two groups: 1. Those of a purely domestic nature. 2. Those of a combined domestic and commercial nature. The domestic books of account included the *libellus familiae*, or *liber patrimonii*, which was kept by the head of the family; the *commentarium*, which was used by the rich as a subsidiary of the first book; and the *kalendarium*, in which were recorded investments, with their dates of maturity and the interests on them.

The books of a combined commercial and domestic nature included the *adversaria*, or *ephemeris*, which was fundamentally a memorandum book, or a first book, and the *codex*, or *tabulae rationum*, the most important account book of the Roman system. The *codex* was in the form of a ledger divided into two pages, one for the income and the other for the outgo. In the *accepti* page, the income, or *accepta* items were entered; in the *expensi* page the outgo, or *expensa* items, were entered. Each page indicated an account, or *ratio*: the *ratio accepti* was the debit, and the *ratio expensi* was the credit. The *codex accepti et expensi* was a legal journal in the form of a bookkeeping memorandum. Since its purpose was to record all written contracts, it was not a true book of account.

From the information now available, there seems to have been no use of double entry, as we know it, during the Roman period, though it may have been present in embryonic form in the Roman bookkeeping system.[1] Double-entry bookkeeping apparently did not come into existence until the rise of medieval commerce.

The most ancient double-entry books known to exist are those of the Massari of the Commune of Genoa, dating from the year 1340. These books are written in perfect double-entry form, which indicates that the system must have been in general use many years before. Commerce, the source of all bookkeeping evolution, had been flourishing at Genoa for a long time, and at this period the city was at the height of her wealth and power. She was exploiting to the full the lucrative Levant trade, and she had humbled her two ancient rivals — Pisa, whom she eliminated as a sea power, and Venice, whom she defeated in naval combats but did not succeed in crushing.

The books of the Commune of Genoa, used by the city to keep account of its finances, consisted of two ledgers: one kept by two Massari, who were the treasury officials of the city, and the other kept by two Maestri Razionali, whose duty it was to watch and check the work of the Massari and keep a duplicate ledger.[2] References are made in these ledgers to transactions of previous years, but all ledgers of previous years are lost, many of them having been destroyed by the Genoese in their uprising in 1339, after the election of the doge Simone Boccanera. Many manuscripts were burnt in Piazza San Lorenzo during the disorder.

This system of double entry probably dates back to 1327, when many reforms were introduced in the Genoese government. At that time, because of *multe fraudes* (many frauds), it was decreed that the *cartulari* (ledgers) were to be kept *ad modum banchi* (after the manner of banks). This, though, cannot be proved directly, for no ledgers of these *banchi* are known to exist.[3] The earliest existing bank records are a ledger and a manual of the Bank of St. George (the forerunner of modern banking) of the year 1408. It is significant that, though this bank began operations as late as 1407, its ledger does not differ in any important aspect from the early *cartulari de'massari*.[4]

Quotations from the ledgers themselves will indicate how these books were kept. An account of Jacobus De Bonicha and a pepper account, *la colonna "Piper,"* are representative examples.[5]

MASSARIA COMMUNIS JANUE DE MCCCXXXX.

MCCCXXXX, *die Vigesima sexta Augusti.*

1. *Jacobus de Bonicha debet nobis pro Anthonio de Marinis valent nobis in isto in* LXI.

    lib. XXXXVIIII, *s.* IIII.

2. *Item die quinta septembris pro Marzocho Pinello valent nobis in isto in* LXXXXII.

    lib. XII, *s.* X.

3. *Item* MCCCXXXXI *die sexta Martij pro alia sua racione valent nobis in alio cartulario novo de* XXXXI *in cartis C.*

    lib. , *s.* XVI.

    SUMMA *lib.* LXII, *s.* X.

MCCCXXXX, *die Vigesima sexta Augusti.*
Recepimus in racione expense Comunis Janue valent nobis in isto in CCXXXI *et sunt pro expensis factis per ipsum Jacobum in exercitu Taxarolii in trabuchis et aliis necessariis pro comuni Janue, et hoc de mandato domini Ducis et sui consilii scripto mano Lanfranchi de Valle notarii* MCCCXXXX *die decimanona augusti.*

    lib. LXII, *s.* X.

August 26, 1340

1. Debit Jacobus de Bonicha and, on page 61, credit Anthonio de Marinis for libbre 49, soldi 4.

2. Item. September 5. Credit Marzocho Pinello, on page 92, for libbre 12, soldi 10.

3. Item. March 6, 1341. Credit his account, on page 100 of the new ledger, for the balance of this account, soldi 16.

TOTAL Libbre 62, soldi 10.

August 26, 1340

Credit Jacobus for disbursements made on behalf of the Commune of Genoa in the army of Taxarolii for ships and other necessities, as shown on page 231 of ledger. These were ordered by the Duke and his council, whose decision was written by the notary Lanfranchi de Valle on August 19, 1340.

Libbre 62, soldi 10.

This is the account of Jacobus de Bonicha taken from page 90 of the ledger. The debits are placed on the left-hand page and the credits on the right-hand page. The title of the account, Jacobus De Bonicha, appears only in the first debit transaction entered in the account.

The phrase *"Jacobus De Bonicha debet nobis . . ."* is a technical one, meaning simply that the account of Jacobus De Bonicha is debited, though the literal translation is, "Jacobus De Bonicha owes us . . ." This phrase is not repeated in subsequent transactions, but is replaced by the word *"item."* In all early ledgers and for a long time thereafter, the debits and credits were distinguished by the use of technical phrases, rather than by the position of entries as in modern ledgers. In the Genoese ledgers, the debits were indicated by the phrases, *"Debet nobis pro . . ."* or *"Debent nobis pro . . ."* The credits, instead, were invariably distinguished by using the phrase *"Recepimus in . . ."* [6] This device originated in the period, before the rise of double entry, when all transactions, whether debits or credits, were listed indiscriminately one after another. A debit or a credit could be recognized as such quickly by a glance at the initial phrase. Similar phrases were used for the same purpose in the Florentine bookkeeping system.[7] Later, when lateral accounts appeared, the distinction between debits and credits became clear from their respective positions, but the old technical phrases continued in use right down to the opening of modern times. Tradition, institutions, and habits do not change abruptly, but stubbornly hang on even though their reasons for existence have long since disappeared.

One of the striking features of these entries in the Massari ledger is their paragraph form. The date, the nature of the transaction, the parties involved, the amount, and the cross reference to other accounts in the ledger are all included in one paragraph. The amount is placed on the right-hand side of the page, but there is no true money column and no date column. The sum total of the debits is placed in the middle of the page at the bottom of the account. The form of the credit side of the account is exactly the same as the debit side, with the exception that the phrase "*Recepimus in . . . ,*" which indicates a credit, is written out only in the first entry and thereafter is replaced by the word "*Item.*" Roman numerals are used throughout, and the ledger is written in Latin, this being the official language of the State.

The account has only one credit, libbre 62, soldi 10, and there are two debits: one of libbre 49, soldi 4, and the other of libbre 12, soldi 10. The third debit of soldi 16 is the balance of the account, which is transferred to page 100 of the new ledger for the incoming year of 1341. The first two debits of the account find their cross-references in the ledger on pages 61 and 92 respectively, as shown in that order below:

MCCCXXXX, *die* IV iulij

Anthonius de Marinis debet nobis pro alia sua ratione, etc.

MCCCXXXX

1. Recepimus, etc.

2. Item die XXVI *augusti accipiendi Jacobo de Bonicha in racione valent nobis in isto in* XC
　　lib. XXXXVIIII, *s.* IIII.

July 4, 1340
Debit Anthonius de Marinis, etc.

1340.

1. Credit, etc.
2. Item. On August 26 credit Jacobus de Bonicha, on page 90, for
　　Libbre 49, soldi 4.

MCCCXXXX

Marzochus Pinellus debet nobis, etc.

MCCCXXXX

1. Recepimus, etc.
2. Item die quinta septembris accipiente Jacobo de Bonicha in racione valent nobis in XC.
　　lib. XII, *s.* X.

1340
Debit Marzochus Pinellus, etc.

1340

1. Credit, etc.
2. Item. On September 5 credit Jacobus de Bonicha, on page 90, for
　　Libbre 12, soldi 10.

The importance of this account is that it affords proof beyond doubt that double entry was known and generally used during this period.

One peculiarity of the Massari ledger is its cross-indexing system. All debits and credits are cross-indexed with the accounts they affect in the ledger, but have no references to original sources. An exception is the cross-reference to accounts in a new ledger at the end of the year, when the old ledger is closed and its accounts transferred. It was general practice in the Middle Ages to open a new ledger every time the old one was closed, whether or not the old one was filled. This cross-indexing system later underwent many changes, which will be explained as they present themselves.

Before proceeding, the monetary system used at Genoa should be explained. The principal monetary unit was the libbra, which was equivalent to 20 soldi, and each soldo was in turn subdivided into 12 denari. It will become evident, before long, that every community had its own money of account, which might differ from all others, a condition which prevailed throughout the Middle Ages. Monetary confusion, with a few exceptions, was a problem with which all governments of the era had constantly to grapple.

The pepper account proves the existence of nominal accounts, a fact of major importance in the origin and evolution of double entry. It is reproduced in full, as follows:

LA COLONNA "PIPER"

MCCCXXXX, *die* VII *Marcii*

1. *Piper Centenaria* LXXX *debent nobis pro Venciguerra Imperiali valent nobis in* VIIII *et sunt pro libris* XXIIII *sol.* V *pro centenario.*

    lib. MDCCCCXXXX.
Censarius Luchas Donatus

2. *Item die* XVII *marcii pro laboratoribus et sunt pro avaria dicti piperis de racione Pachalis de Furneto valent nobis in* VIIII *bis. s.* XIIII.

3. *Item ea die accipiente Anthonio de Framura garbellatore, pro garbellaturis dicti piperis centenaria* XXXXI *de racione dicti Paschalis, valent nobis in* VIIII.

    lib.   , *s.* X, *d.* IIII.

MCCCXXXX, *die* XII *Marcii*

1. *Recepimus in vendea de centariis dicti piperis in Joanne de Franco de Florentia, el pro eo in racione Cristiani Lomellini, valent nobis in* III. *lib.* CCXXVII, *s.* V. *et sunt pro libr.* XXII, *sol.* XIIII, *d.* VI *ad numeratum.*

2. *Item die* XXX *marcii in vendea de centenario uno piperis in Jacobo Maria de Querio, et pro eo in racione anthonii de Recho, notarii, valent nobis in* XIIII *pro libr.* XXII, *s.* X.

    lib. XXII, *s.* X.

3. *Item ea die in vendea de centen.* XV *et* III *quar. piperis pro libris* XXII, *sol.* X *pro centenario, in Jacobo Tauso de Mediolano et pro Paschale de Furneto, valent nobis in* X.

    lib. CCCLIIII, *s.* VII, *d.* VI.

4. Item die Marcii pro sachi XIIII *et pro garbellaturis dicti piperis deracione dicti Paschalis, valent nobis in* X.
 lib. II, *s.* IIII, *d.* IIII.

5. Item ea die ponderaturis piperis de racione dicti Paschalis valent nobis in X *termino Kalend. iulii.*
 lib. , *s.* X, *d.* VIII.

6. Item quia scribi debebatur usque die VII *marcii pro centenariis* IIII *et libris* XII 1/2 *dicti piperis, pro libr.* XXIIII *solo* V *pro centenario, de racione ven ciguerre Imperialis in* VIII.
 lib. C, *s.* VI.

7. Item ea die pro ripa totius piperis centenarii LXXXXIIII *et libre* XII 1/10 *de racione dicti Venciguerre in* VIIII.
 lib. XXV, *s.* , *d.* X.

8. Item ea die pro sachi XX *dicti Piperis de racione dicti venciguerre in* VIIII.
 lib. II, *s.* III, *d.* IIII.

9. Item die VIII *Aprilis pro certis avariis dicti piperis de racione piperis valent nobis in* LXXIIII.
 lib. I, *s.* X, *d.* X.
SUMMA libre IILXXIII, *s.* IIII.

4. Item ea in vendea de centinariis II *pro libr.* XXII, *sol* X, *in Petro Bordino de Ast, et pro eo in Paschale de Furneto valent nobis in* X.
 lib. XXXXV.

5. Item die predicta pro pluribus centenariis piperis in racione vendea dicti piperis valent nobis in isto antea in presenti carta LXXIII.
 lib. MCCLXXIII, *s.* VIIII, *d.* VI.

6. Item die VII *novembris in dampno centenariorum* LXXXIIII *et libri* XII 1/10 *dicti piperis in racione proventium in isto* XXXVII.
 lib. CXXXVIIII, *s.* XII.
SUMMA libre IILXXIII, *s.* IIII.

March 7, 1340.
1. Debit eighty 100-lb. lots of pepper and credit, on page 9, Venciguerre Imperiali; pepper priced at 24 libbre and 5 soldi per 100-lb. lot.
 Libbre 1,940.
Government broker Luchas Donatus.

2. Item. March 17. Credit, on page 9, Paschalis de Furneto for labor and damaged pepper.
 Soldi 14.

March 12, 1340.
1. Credit pepper and debit, on page 3, Cristiani Lomellini for pepper sold him for the account of Joanne de Franco of Florence, at the price of 22 libbre, 14 soldi, 6 denari per 100-lb. lot.
 Libbre 227, soldi 5.

2. Item. March 30. Debit, on page 14, Anthonii de Recho, notary, for 100-lb. lot sold to him for the account of Jacobo Maria de Querio, at the price of 22 libbre, soldi 10.
 Libbre 22, soldi 10.

3. Item. March 17. Credit, on page 9. Paschalis for tax to be paid to tax collector, Anthonio de Framura, on 41 lots of pepper.

Soldi 10, denari 4.

4. Item. March 17. Credit, on page 10, Paschalis for tax on 14 lots of pepper.

Libbre 2, soldi 4, denari 4.

5. Item. March 17. Credit, on page 10, Paschalis for the weighing of pepper.

Soldi 10, denari 8.

6. Item. Credit Venciguerre Imperialis, on page 8, for obligations owing him up to March 7 for 4 lots and 12 1/2 lbs. of pepper, amounting to 24 libbre and 5 soldi per lot.

Libbre 100, soldi 6.

7. Item. March 17. Credit Venciguerre, on page 9, for the cost of unloading the entire cargo of 94 100-lb. lots and 12 1/10 lbs. of pepper.

Libbre 25, denari 10.

8. Item. March 17. Credit, on page 9, Venciguerre for 20 lots of pepper.

Libbre 2, soldi 3, denari 4.

9. Item. April 8. Credit, on page 74, the account of pepper damages for losses sustained.

Libbre 1, soldi 10, denari 10.

TOTAL   Libbre 2,073, soldi 4.

3. Item. March 30. Debit Jacobo Tauso de Mediolano, through Paschale de Furneto's account on page 10, for 15 3/4 lots of pepper sold him at 22 libbre, soldi 10 per lot.

Libbre 354, soldi 7, denari 6.

4. Item. March 30. Debit Petro Bordino de Ast, through Paschale de Furneto's account on page 10, for 2 lots sold him at 22 libbre, 10 soldi per lot.

Libbre 45.

5. Item. March 30. Debit, on this same page 73, the account sale of pepper for the balance of 100-lb. pepper lots.

Libbre 1,237, soldi 9, denari 6.

6. Item. November 7. Debit profit-and-loss account, on page 37, for the loss incurred on the venture of 84 hundred-lb. lots and 12 1/10 lbs. of pepper.

Libbre 149, soldi 12.

TOTAL   Libbre 2,073, soldi 4.

This is a typical venture account of the Middle Ages. The Commune of Genoa took a flyer in pepper. It purchased eighty 100-pound lots of this merchandise, which presumably had just arrived from the Orient, at a cost of 24 libbre and 5 soldi per lot, and then, with economic acumen common to most governments, disposed of it at the price of 22 libbre and 10 soldi per 100-pound lot, sustaining a considerable loss.

The account is necessarily of a mixed nature. It includes the purchase of pepper and all its incidental expenses, the sales, and the loss incurred on the whole venture. It clearly illustrates the medieval method of profit-and-loss calculation. Every venture, whether it was the purchase of a batch of goods or the fitting out of one or more ships for a commercial trip to the Orient, was thought of as a unit; separate accounts were opened for each. These accounts were debited with their costs and credited with their sales, and the balance naturally showed the profits or losses made on each separate venture. At the termination of the venture, the account was closed by transferring the balance to a general profit-and-loss account.

The significance of this pepper account lies in the fact that it is the first to show a systematic use of a profit-and-loss account in a double-entry framework.

The cross-entry postings of the six credits of the account are as follows:

Debit page	Credit page
Fol. 3	MCCCXXXX
(*N.B. — This is the account of Giovanni Franco of Florence, but because of dampness the page has deteriorated to the extent that it is now illegible.*)	*Recepimus, etc.*
	Summa, etc.
	1340
	Credit, etc.
	Total, etc.
Fol. 14	
MCCCXXXX, *die X martii*	*Recepimus, etc.*
1. Anthonius de Recho notarius debet nobis pro Jacobo Maria de Querio pro centenario uno Piperis de racione dicti piperis valent nobis in LXXIII.	
lib. XXII, *s.* X.	
Summa, etc.	*Summa, etc.*
Page 14	
1340, March 10.	
1. Debit Anthonius de Recho, notary, and credit pepper, on page 73, for 100-lb. lot for the account of Jacobo Maria de Querio.	Credit, etc.
Libbre 22, soldi 10.	
Total, etc.	Total, etc.

Fol. 10

MCCCXXXX

1. *Pasquale de Furneto debet nobis,*   *Recepimus, etc.*
etc.

2. *Item die XXX marcii pro Jacobo
Tauso de Mediolano et sunt pro centenariis XVIII piperis pro lib. XXII, sol.
X, pro centenario de racione diĉti
piperis valent nobis in LXXIII.*
    lib. CCCLIIII, s. VII, d. VI.

3. *Item ea die pro Petro de Aĉt et sunt
pro centenariis II piperis pro libr.
XXII, sol. X, pro centenario, de racione
diĉti piperis in LXXIII.*
    lib. XXXXV.
    Summa, etc.   *Summa, etc.*

Page 10

1340

1. Debit Pasquale de Furneto, etc.   Credit, etc.

2. Item. March 30. Credit pepper, on
page 73, for 18 lots of pepper bought
for the account of Jacobo Tauso de
Mediolano at 22 libbre, soldi 10 per
lot.
    Libbre 354, soldi 7, denari 6.

3. Item. March 30. Credit pepper, on
page 73, for two lots of pepper bought
for the account of Petro de Aĉt at 22
libbre, soldi 10 per lot.
    Libbre 45.
    Total, etc.   Total, etc.

Fol. 73

MCCCXXXX *die XXX Martii*
1. *Vendea piperis debet nobis, etc.*   *Recepimus, etc.*

2. *Item ea die pro ratione piperis valent
nobis in iĉto retro in presenti cartis
LXXIII.*
    lib. MCCLXXIII, s. VIIII, d. VI.
    Summa, etc.   *Summa, etc.*

Page 73

1340, March 30.	
1. Debit sale of pepper, etc.	Credit, etc.
2. Item. March 30. Credit the above pepper account, on this same page 73. Libbre 1,237, soldi 9, denari 6.	
Total, etc.	Total, etc.

Fol. 37

MCCCXXXX, *die X Marcii*	
1. *Proventus cambii et dampnum de rauba vendita debet nobis, etc.*	*Recepimus, etc.*
2. *Item ea die (7 novembris) pro dampno . . . (illegible)*	
Summa, etc.	*Summa, etc.*

Page 37

1340, March 10	
1. Debit profit-and-loss account and credit pepper account for loss incurred on the sale.	Credit, etc.
2. Item. On same day (Nov. 7) for loss. . . .	
Total, etc.	Total, etc.

The cross entries of the pepper account:

Fol. 9

MCCCXXXX	MCCCXXXX, *die VII Marcij*
Venciguerre Imperialis debet nobis, etc.	1. *Recepimus in pipere centenaria* LXXX *pro libris* XXIIII, *sol* V *iannuinorum pro centenario valent nobis in* XXXII.
	lib. MDCCCCXXXX.
	TERMINO (?) *die* VII *iulii.*
Summa, etc.	*Summa, etc.*

Page 9

1340
Debit Venciguerre Imperialis, etc.

1340 March 7

1. Credit this account and debit pepper for eighty 100-lb. lots of pepper, on page 37, at 24 libbre, 5 soldi per 100-lb. lot.

Libbre 1,940.

July 7

Total, etc.

Total, etc.

Fol. 9

MCCCXXXX
Pasquale de Furneto debet nobis, etc.

MCCCXXXX

1. *Recepimus, etc.*

2. *It. die XVII marcij laboratoribus pro avaria piperis in racione dicti piperis valent nobis in LXXII.*
lib. , s. XIIII.

3. *It. ea die accipiente Anthonio de Framura garbellatore in racione dicti piperis valent nobis in LXXVIII.* (*This account is damaged and not very legible, but it is sufficiently understandable to be sure that it is the cross entry corresponding to that in the pepper account.*)

Summa, etc.

Summa, etc.

Page 9

1340
Debit Pasquale de Furneto, etc.

1340

1. Credit, etc.

2. Item. March 7. Debit pepper account, on page 73, for labor and damaged pepper, soldi 14.

3. Item. March 7. Debit pepper, on page 73, for tax collected by Anthonio de Framura.

Total, etc.

Total, etc.

Fol. 10

<table>
<tr><td>MCCCXXXX
Pasquale de Furneto debet nobis, etc.</td><td>MCCCXXXX
1. Recepimus, etc.</td></tr>
</table>

Fol. 10
MCCCXXXX
Pasquale de Furneto debet nobis, etc.

MCCCXXXX

1. Recepimus, etc.

*2. . . . pro sachi XIV pro garbella-
turis dicti piperis centen. XXI et pro
laboratoribus in racione dicti piperis
valent nobis.*

lib. II, s. IIII, d. IIII.

*3. It. usque die XX marcij pro ponde-
raturis piperis in racioni dicti piperis,
valent nobis in LXXIII.*

lib.   , s. X, d. IIII.

Summa, etc.   *Summa, etc.*

Page 10

1340
Debit Pasquale de Furneto, etc.

1340
1. Credit, etc.

2. . . . debit pepper for tax and labor
on 14 bags of pepper.

Libbre 2, soldi 4, denari 4.

3. Item. Debit pepper, on page 73, for
the weighing of the pepper up to March
20.

Soldi 10, denari 4.

Total, etc.   Total, etc.

Fol. 8

MCCCXXXX
Venciguerra Imperialis debet nobis, etc.   *Recepimus, etc.*

Summa, etc.   *Summa, etc.*

Page 8

1340
Debit Venciguerra Imperialis, etc.   Credit, etc.
Total, etc.   Summa, etc.

Fol. 9
MCCCXXXX
Venciguerra Imperialis debet nobis, etc.

1. *Recepimus, etc.*

2. *It. ea die* (VII *marcij*) *pro ripa dicti piperis in racione dicti piperis in* LXXIII.
   lib. XXV, *s.* X.

3. *It. ea die pro sachi* XX *dicti piperis in racione dicti piperis in* LXXIII.
   lib. II, *s.* III, *d.* IIII.
   Summa, etc.

Summa, etc.

Page 9
1340
Debit Venciguerra Imperialis, etc.

1. Credit, etc.

2. Item. On same date (March 7), debit pepper, on page 73, for the unloading of pepper.
   Libbre 25, soldi 10.

3. Item. March 7. Debit pepper, on page 73, for 20 lots of pepper.
   Libbre 2, soldi 3, denari 4.
   Total, etc.

Total, etc.

Fol. 74
MCCCXXXX, *die* XXX *Martis*
Avarie piperis et aliis debent nobis etc.

MCCCXXXX, *die* VIII *aprilis.*
Recepimus in racione piperis valent nobis in isto in LXXIII.
Lib. I, *s.* X, *d.* X.
Summa, etc.

Summa, etc.

Page 74
1340, March 30
Debit damages for pepper and, etc.

1340, April 8.
Debit, on this same page 73, the account of pepper.
Libbre 1, soldi 10, denari 10.
Total, etc.

Total, etc.

ORIGIN AND EVOLUTION OF DOUBLE ENTRY BOOKKEEPING

It is now clear that double-entry bookkeeping was fully developed at Genoa in 1340, and it is also clear that its origin must have been of a considerably earlier date. It is inconceivable that a system such as double entry should come into being suddenly in the mature form shown in the Massari ledgers; it could only have evolved gradually over a long period of time. The double-entry system used by the Commune of Genoa dates back probably no further than 1327, when the government decreed that its accounts were to be kept in the same way as banks kept their accounts. Thus, as it has already been stated above, the origin of the system must be sought in the phenomenon of that general rise of commerce characteristic of the era of the Communes and the Renaissance.

NOTES

[1] Bariola, Plinio. *Storia della ragioneria italiana* (Milano, Cavalli, 1897), part 2, pp. 229–240.

Many erroneously believe that Roman culture was completely destroyed by invasions of barbarians. To the contrary, the culture of the Romans was accepted by the barbarians, and though greatly retarded in its progress, continued throughout the Middle Ages. The Roman bookkeeping system also continued in use, since it fulfilled the important function of keeping the proprietor informed of his financial position. To say that the Roman bookkeeping system disappeared is tantamount to saying that its principal cause of existence also disappeared, that is, that private property disappeared, and this is not the case. (See Dopsch, A., *Grundlagen der europäischen kulturentwicklung* (Vienna, 1923), vols. 1 and 2 — especially vol. 2, pp. 402–502; and his *Wirtschaftsentwicklung der karolingerzeit* (Weimar, 1922), especially vol. 2.)

The following three facts should be sufficient proof of the continuity of the Roman bookkeeping system:

1. The Roman landed domain continued in the early Middle Ages to constitute the basic element of the feudal organization. The practical problem of accounting, therefore, had not changed. The German conquerors did not supplant the Romans entirely, but in most instances took but a third or two-thirds of the land, and it is certain also that they hired many Romans to handle their business affairs. It is safe to assume that these Romans employed the Roman system of accounts.
2. In the Justinian Code of 529–534 A.D., one still finds mention of the ancient *codex accepti et expensi*, indicating a continuity in portions of the empire not conquered by the Germans. This code became the law of the Roman inhabitants of Italy during the years 555–568 A.D.
3. When Charlemagne reorganized the administration of his reign, he engaged Italian teachers of abacus to help him. Though primarily teachers of arithmetic, they also taught the art of keeping books. (Bariola. Op. cit., part 2, chap. 6, p. 249, and all of part 1.)

Thus it is logical to suppose that the *codex rationum, adversaria, kalendarium*, and *commentarium* continued in use after the fall of the western Roman Empire.

[2] Besta, Fabio. *La ragioneria* (Milano, Vallardi, 1922–29), vol. 3, p. 273. "*Questi registri a partita doppia . . . sono due cartulari o maltri in pergamena, l'uno dei massari, l'altro de'maeltri razionali del commune di Genova. I massari, due in numero, curavano la massaria o, come direbbesi ora, l'azienda o le finanze del commune; i maeltri razionali, pure due in numero, avevano la vigilanza e il riscontro sull'opera dei massari e dei loro dipendenti.*"

16

[3] It may be that the *banchi* operated after the manner of the *changeors* of the Champagne fairs. (See Bourquelot, F., *Etudes sur les Foires de Champagne*, vol. 2, pp. 352 et seq.) It was the practice of merchants who gathered at the fairs to deposit their funds with money changers for the duration of the fair and to pay for purchases by having the money changers transfer their money to the account of their creditors. The money changers recorded such transactions on wax tablets, which showed the amount of money received, transferred, and paid out. Similar tablets were kept by the merchants, so that their entries would correspond with those of the money changers.

The fact that the government of Genoa issued a law that its bookkeeping records be kept in the manner of these *banchi* might indicate that double entry was used at the fairs. But no records exist by which the origin of double entry can be traced definitely to this source.

[4] Besta, Fabio. Op. cit., vol. 3, bk. 9, chap. 9, art. I.

[5] These two examples are taken from Bariola's *Storia della ragioneria italiana*, part 2, chap. 11; Bariola has himself quoted them from Desimoni, whose conclusions regarding Genoese double entry he has summarized as follows:

a As early as the beginning of the fourteenth century, the Commune requested that the books be kept after the manner of banks;

b All erasures and blank spaces in the ledgers were prohibited;

c Before being put into use, every ledger had to have its pages numbered and a statement inserted at the beginning of the book showing in what manner the ledger was to be kept;

d Errors were not to be cancelled, but to be made right by proper debit and credit operations bringing about the proper balance;

e The books were replaced yearly, the balances of the old ledger being transferred to the new ledger;

f Changes of property, obligations, etc., were transcribed from the main ledger to the respective subsidiary books;

g Even from the beginning of the fourteenth century, there was a sharp distinction between the ledger and the journal;

h Document 3, quoted by Desimoni, proves the duplication of entries;

i Document 4 shows, besides the duplication of entries, how a loss of 84 centenari and 12 libbre was sustained in the pepper account and transferred to a profit-and-loss account.

Observations *h* and *i* prove beyond doubt the double-entry form of the two Massari ledgers.

[6] Besta. Op. cit., vol. 3, bk. 9, chap. 9, art. 1.

[7] Ceccherelli, Alberto. *Le scritture commerciali nelle antiche aziende fiorentine* (Firenze, Lastrucci, 1910), chap. 3, pp. 30–33.

Corsani. Op. cit., chap. 2, p. 45.

Chapter II

FLORENCE

HE vigorous and growing Florentine commerce of the thirteenth and fourteenth centuries was exceptionally well suited for the development of bookkeeping. This was a period of great prosperity. The movement, begun in the twelfth century, which transformed the old agricultural and feudal city into a city of merchants and bankers was then completed. During the last two centuries, Florence had been slowly gaining prestige by the manufacture and sale of her cloth throughout Europe and by establishing herself as the foremost banking center of Western Europe. She avoided the general confusion and multiplicity of monetary systems. In 1252 she coined for the first time the gold florin (fiorino d'oro), which soon was accepted as the standard gold piece throughout Europe, enhancing immeasurably her prestige and commercial advantage over all competitors.

One great achievement of the commercial genius of the Florentines was the development of large associations and *compagnie* (partnerships), units which began with the pooling of capital within family groups and only gradually developed to the point of admitting outside capital. Ultimately the family aspect of partnerships disappeared entirely.

At this stage, Florentine partnerships possessed great power and wealth. In 1338, Villani says there were 80 powerful *compagnie*, and a few years later Peruzzi says that these had increased to 108.[1]

The outburst of commercial and industrial activity brought a great accumulation of wealth, which fostered the art of exchange, an art which the Florentines mastered so well that they became in a short while the leading bankers of Europe. A city such as Florence, where the arts and sciences were fostered to the same extent as the accumulation of wealth through commercial enterprises, was ideal for the development of the arts closely allied to commerce. Such an art is bookkeeping.[2] The greater abundance of early manuscripts, too, makes it easier to trace the evolution of bookkeeping in Florence than in either Genoa or Venice. The account books of the Peruzzi, Bardi, Del Bene, Datini, and others cover the whole of the fourteenth century and throw much light on the origin of double entry.

Even before Florence became an industrial and commercial city, it was common practice there to keep a memorandum book, called *ricordanze*, in which the most important facts of the day were jotted down. These memorandum records are perhaps the most ancient commercial documents existing in Italy after the fall of the Roman Empire. The earliest bears the date of 1211. They were used, as has been said, to record any fact which the writer thought important — a political or social event, a defeat or a victory, a commercial transaction or other financial matter. Therefore, as commercial records, they are of the most simple form possible, the narrative form.[3]

More important records, for the student of double entry, do not appear until the fourteenth century, when the remarkable growth of large Florentine *compagnie* compelled the development of account books peculiar to Florence. The *compagnie* also developed the partnership contract to a remarkable degree of perfection. Their contracts clearly stated the capital of all the separate partners; made provisions for the division of profits and losses; clearly defined the rights and duties of each partner; and finally provided for the dissolution of the *compagnie*. Upon this solid foundation, the *compagnie* proceeded to open *i libri delle ragioni*, the books of account.[4]

The Florentine account books of the fourteenth century may be divided into two groups, each one having a distinctly different account form: the first includes all which appeared up to 1380, and the second includes those of the remaining two decades. Accounts of the first group are cast in the form which is characteristic of the early Florentine commercial manuscripts. The debit and credit sections are placed one above the other, instead of on opposite pages, as at Genoa and Venice. At the top of the page appeared whichever section chanced to open the account: uniformity in the placing of debit and credit was impossible. The chief characteristic of the second group was the introduction, from Venice, of lateral accounts into the bookkeeping framework of Florence. The full significance of this innovation will be seen later on.[5]

At the beginning of the fourteenth century, a distinction was already being made between principal and secondary books[6] of account — a distinction, though, that was not as yet definite and clear-cut, since bookkeeping did not at the start have a well rounded theory, but was the natural outcome of commercial activity and efforts of merchants to solve problems forced upon them by the increasing complexity of trade.[7]

Monetary values were regularly expressed by Tuscan firms in fiorini, soldi, and denari, or fiorini, lire[8], and denari, and sometimes in lire, soldi, and denari. The fiorino d'oro was first coined in the year 1252; its value was equivalent to twenty soldi, each of which equaled twelve denari. Gradually other types of fiorini came into existence, such as the fiorino di suggello, fiorino di galea, fiorino stretto, fiorino di camera, fiorino d'oro largo in oro, and fiorino a fiorino. The lira, as a coin, first appeared in Florence during the time of Cosimo I de'Medici.[9]

To demonstrate better the changes occurring in Florentine bookkeeping during the fourteenth century, abstracts from Peruzzi's ledger of 1336 and from the numerous Datini ledgers covering the period from 1366 to 1386 will be presented. The ledger began in 1336 with a *bilancio* (balance account) of the old *compagnia* for the years 1331–1335. It was characteristic of this early period to open all ledgers with a balance account. This account included all the assets and liabilities, and it served exactly the same purpose as the *introito* account described by Venetian writers almost two centuries later.[10] The *bilancio* covers ten pages of the Peruzzi ledger. Only portions of it will be quoted below: [11]

	addì i Luglio MCCCXXXV	*fiorino d'oro*	*soldi*	*denari*
C	*Giotto de'Peruzzi e Compagni di Vecchia Compagnia che cominciò in 1 Luglio MCCCXXXI e finì in 1 Luglio MCCCXXXV ci devono dare dì 1 di Luglio milletrecentotrentacinque affior. demo per loro a Giotto Arnoldo de'Peruzzi per quarta parte ed a Rinieri di Pacino de'Peruzzi e a fratelli e nipoti per l'altra quarta parte e a Bonifazio e a Tommaso de'Peruzzi per l'atra quarta parte ed a Berto di M. Ridolfo de' Peruzzi ed a fratelli per l'altra quarta parte ponemo che devono avere nel CXXXV.*	MDCCCL		
C (a)	*Deono dare dì 1 Luglio anno MCCCXXXV affiorini demo a Tommaso di Filippo di Pacino de'Peruzzi dee avere CXXXVIII.*	CCCCLXXX	VIII	I
C (b)	*Deono dare dì 1 Luglio anno MCCCXXXV affiorini demo a Rinieri e Tommaso di Pacino de'Peruzzi ciascuno per terza parte e a Donato figliolo del detto Pacino e Giovanni e Francesco figlioli de Salvestro per l'altra terza parte ponemo che dee avere nel CXXXVIII.*	LV	XII	X

July 1, 1335.

		fiorino d'oro	*soldi*	*denari*
C	Debit Giotto de'Peruzzi and partners of the old company, which began July 1, 1331, and ended July 1, 1335, for *affiorini* apportioned as follows: Debit Giotto Arnoldo de'Peruzzi for 1/4, debit Rinieri di Pacino de'Peruzzi and brothers and nephews for 1/4, debit Bonifazio and Tommaso de'Peruzzi for 1/4, and debit Berto di M. Ridolfo de'Peruzzi and brothers for the other 1/4, which are credited on page 135.	1,850		
C (a)	Debit, on July 1, 1335, Tommaso di Filippo di Pacino de'Peruzzi for *affiorini*, which is credited on page 138.	490	8	2
C (b)	Debit, on July 1, 1335, Rinieri and Tommaso di Pacino de'Peruzzi each 1/3, and debit Donato, son of Pacino, and Giovanni and Francesco, sons of Salvestro, for the other 1/3, which are credited on page 138.	55	12	10

Each of these debit entries bears cross-reference numbers of their credit entries. Two of the credit entries appear on page 138 of the ledger:

(a)   MCCCXXXV *addì 1 Luglio*   CCCCLXXXX   VIII   II

Tommaso di Filippo di Pacino de'Peruzzi dee avere kl. luglio anno 1335 aff. per Giotto Peruzzi e Compagni di vecchia compagnia che cominciò in kl. Luglio 1331 e finì in kl. Luglio 1335. Posto che ci deono dare nel II.

(b)   MCCCXXXV *addì 1 Luglio*   LV   XII

Rinieri e Tommaso figliolo che furono Pacino de'Peruzzi ciascuno per terza parte e Donato figliolo che fu del detto Pacino e Giovanni e Francesco figlioli che furono di Salvestro del detto Pacino e Pacino figliolo che fu di Benedetto di Pacino de'Peruzzi soparadetto per la loro terza parte deono avere kl. Luglio anno 1335 a fiorini per Giotto de'Peruzzi e Compagni de vecchia compagnia che cominiciò in Luglio 1331 e finì in Luglio 1335 ponemo che ci deono dare nel II in questo libro e deglino li levarono ove i sopradetti dovevano avere a loro libro dell'asse quinto nel dugentotrentasette.

July 1, 1335

(a) Credit Tommaso di Filippo di Pacino de'Peruzzi,   490   8   2
on July 1, 1335, for *affiorini*, and debit, on page 2, Giotto Peruzzi and partners of the old company, which began July 1, 1331, and ended July 1, 1335.

(b)   July 1, 1335
Credit, on July 1, 1335, Rinieri and Tommaso,   55   12
sons of the late Pacino de'Peruzzi, each for 1/3, and credit Donato, son of the late Pacino, and credit Giovanni and Francesco, sons of the late Salvestro, son of the deceased Pacino, and credit Pacino (Jr.), son of the late Benedetto, son of the deceased Pacino de'Peruzzi (Sr.), for the other 1/3, and debit, on page 2, Giotto de'Peruzzi and partners of the old company, which began July 1, 1331, and ended July, 1335.

The capital structure of the partnership is clearly stated in the above *bilancio*. The total capital of 1,850 fiorini a oro is divided equally among four partners, who in turn divide their share among subpartners. The account form is the vertical one characteristic of early Florentine bookkeeping. The debit and credit entries are definitely tied together by a cross-index system. There is a crude money column to the right of the account, and though money values are stated in Roman numerals, arabic numerals are beginning to be used for other informal figures.

21

Leonardo Fibonacci introduced the arabic numerals in Florence in 1202, and yet, 133 years later, the new and far superior numerical system had made but little headway, another instance of the persistency of habits and institutions.

On page 112 of the same Peruzzi ledger there is the expense account quoted below:

Spese

MCCCXXXVII *addì 1 Luglio*

Bonifazio Peruzzi e Compagni di nostra compagnia ci deono dare da dì 1 Luglio MCCCXXXVII i quali doniamo a Madonna Nice figliola de Lupo de Ghiberti per guadagno di una sua ragione fino a detto dì ponemo avere nel cl.	LVIIII
Deono dare 1 Luglio MCCCXXXVII i quali donammo per loro a Manno di Lippo de'Gherardini per guadagno di una sua ragione.	CXXXVIIII

Expenses

July 1, 1337

Debit on July 1, 1337, Bonifazio Peruzzi and partners of our company, and credit, on page 150, Madonna Nice, daughter of Lupo de Ghiberti, for a profit on her account up to this day.	59
Debit the above on July 1, 1337, and credit Manno di Lippo de'Gherardini for a profit on his account.	139

All profits were transferred to an account called *avanzi*, which is missing. The existence of a profit-and-loss account in this ledger is of great importance. One cannot conclusively say, however, that double entry was in use at Florence at this time, because there are many missing and torn pages which included accounts such as the profit-and-loss. Still, the Peruzzi ledger has many double-entry characteristics. This is of great importance, for it precedes by five years the Massari ledgers of 1340 of the Commune of Genoa.[12]

The Datini ledgers are far more complete and have an uninterrupted continuity, running from 1366 to 1410. The bookkeeping technique of the Datini *compagnia* underwent great changes, the most outstanding being the gradual substitution of lateral accounts for the vertical ones. The first to undergo this change were the accounts of debtors and creditors, and gradually all the other accounts were affected.

This evolution is best seen by comparing abstracts from the first Datini ledger of the Avignon branch with abstracts from the 1383 ledger of the Pisa branch, when lateral accounts were first introduced.

The earliest of Datini's ledgers was kept at Avignon and had a fiscal period of one year. The ledger was opened in 1366 and was closed in 1367. The following abstracts are taken from this ledger. [13]

22

MCCCLXVJ   xxviiij *di diciembre*

Gli osti nostri della chasa e della bottegha che tengnamo da lloro in Vignone
deono dare dì xxiiij di diciembre 1366; levamo dal quaderno roso delle
richordanze da carte xliij dove dare doveano per una ragione iscritta in iij
partite in somma fiorini cinquant'otto d'oro di gralli a soldi xiiij provenzali.
                                        fior. lxx, s. xj, d. o.

Posto in questo libro innanzi a carte cciij a piè d'una loro ragione dove avere
doveano per magiore soma ponemo a piè ch'avesono autto per questa
ragione, però daniamo di quì.   *fior. lxx, s. xj, d. o prov.*

December 29, 1366

Debit on December 24, 1366, the landlords of our Avignon branch for three
transactions, which were taken from page 43 of the red memorandum
book, for the amount of 58 fiorini d'oro di gralli, each valued at 14
soldi provenzali.   fior. 70, soldi 11, denari o.

Credit the landlords and debit the landlords' payable account, on page 203, to
offset a larger amount due them for rent.   fior. 70, s. 11, d. o prov.

MCCCLXVJ   dì xviiij *di diciembre*

Gli osti nostri della chasa e della bottegha che tengniamo da lloro in Vignone
deono avere dì xxxj di diciembre 1366 per pigione di detta chasa e
botegha cioè da dì xiij di Luglio MCCCLXIII, insino a sopradetto dì
xxxj di diciembre MCCCLXVI che sono anni tre, mesi cinque, die
diciotto, per pregio di fiorini ventisette d'oro di grali per ano; monta in
soma fiorini novantatre d'oro di grali e soldi venti e denari quatro
provenzali.   *fior. cxij, s. xij, d. iiij prov.*

Anone autto, levamo di questo libro adietro da carte viij, dove dare doveano per
una ragione in soma fiorini lxx, soldi xj provenzali; danamo, ch'avesono
datto.   *fior. lxx, s. xj, d. o prov.*

December 29, 1366

Credit the landlords of our Avignon branch on December 31, 1366, for rent due
them on their store and house for the period starting July 13, 1363, and
ending December 31, 1366, that is, 3 years, 5 months, and 18 days, at the
yearly rate of 27 fiorini d'oro di grali, which amounts to 93 fiorini d'oro
di grali, 20 soldi, and 4 denari provenzali.   fior. 112, s. 12, d. 4 prov.

Debit the landlords and credit the same on page 8 for the balance of that receivable account, which is applied against this payable account.
                                        fior. 70, s. 11, d. o prov.

These are two accounts: the first is an account receivable, and the second an account payable. Both are of the same party, the landlords of the house and store (*gli osti della chasa e della bottegha*). The account receivable, being the smaller of the two amounts, is closed into the account payable, and only the net amount is shown as due to the landlords. These are two typical vertical accounts.[14] The relative position of debits and credits is not fixed, for one account begins with a debit and the other with a credit, making necessary the use of artificial phrases to distinguish them from each other. As a rule, the first entry of the top section of every account begins with the title of the account, followed by either *dee dare* or *deono dare* for those starting with debits, and by *dee avere* or *deono avere* for those starting with credits. The title is not repeated in any of the subsequent entries of either section. All the succeeding entries of the top section begin directly with *dee dare* or *deono dare*, and with *dee avere* or *deono avere*. All entries of the bottom section, including the initial one, begin with *anne avuto* or *annone avuto* for debits, and with *anne dato* or *annone dato* for credits. It must be remembered that the bottom section of an account is always the opposite, in debit and credit, from the top section.

There are other noteworthy characteristics: A crude money column is placed to the right of the account, with values written in Roman numerals. Arabic numerals are used in the text of the entry. A fairly well developed cross-index system ties together the debit and credit ledger entries, differing, however, from the indexing system of the *Massari* ledgers in that the entries themselves indicate the memorandum books from which they originate.

The time was ripe for the introduction of lateral accounts. The Florentine system of double entry was now fully developed. Assets, liabilities, and nominal and capital accounts were all included in the bookkeeping framework. The entries were analyzed as to their debits and credits, and a *bilancio* (balance-sheet), which will be described later, was correctly drawn up and made the basis for the determination and division of profits among the partners.

It was upon this system, developed entirely by Florentine merchants, that the Venetian lateral accounts were grafted. In the subsequent examples it will be seen more clearly that double entry was not imported from Venice, as many believed, but was developed at Florence independently. Lateral accounts only were taken from the Venetian bookkeeping system, but the use made of this device proved most advantageous.

Lateral accounts, as far as is known, first appeared in Tuscany in 1382 in the *vacchetta* (memorandum book) of an unknown Paliano di Folco Paliani of Pisa. Only the ledger accounts for debtors and creditors were divided laterally, and the ledger entries were not cross-indexed.

An example will illustrate this.[15]

1382
Bartolomeo Chatanelli de'dare a dì 13 di dicenbre li demmo constanti fior. sesanta in suggello. fior. 60

1382
Bartolomeo Chatanelli de'avere a dì 14 di dicenbre; ci die in moneta fior. sessanta. fior. 60

1382
Debit Bartolomeo Chatanelli on December 13 for 60 fiorini in suggello. fior. 60

1382
Credit Bartolomeo Chatanelli on December 14 for 60 fiorini. fior. 60

This *vacchetta* is also important for another reason: Paliano di Folco Paliani, in using this new account form, says in his heading that he is adopting the Venetian method of placing the debit on one page and the credit on the opposite page (*scritto alla viniziana, cioè ne l'una carta dare e dirimpetto avere*). This established the fact that lateral accounts were introduced into Tuscany from Venice and grafted upon a preëxisting system of remote origin, which had developed according to the circumstances and needs it had to satisfy.[16]

The most ancient Datini ledger using lateral accounts also appeared at Pisa. A new branch of the Datini Compagnia was opened at that city in 1383, lasting until 1408. Datini may have known of Paliano's *vacchetta* of the previous year, because the ledger of this new branch also has lateral accounts for debtors and creditors only. All other accounts were still vertically divided. This will be illustrated by a few examples. An account payable:[17]

c. lxxxxjt
Nicholò di Francesco e Fratelli di Firenze de'dare a dì xvj di maggio fior. quatrociento d., demo per lui a Messer Banducio Bonchonti; portò Simone di Francescho a uscita b. ac. 132. fior. cccc, d. .

E deono dare a dì xxx d'aghosto fior. cientocinquanta, s. sedici, denari otto a oro, demo per lui a Messer Banducio Bonchonti, portò Francescho di Bartolomeo, a uscita b. ac. 143. fior. cl, s. xvj, d. viij, o.
550/16/8

c. lxxxxij
Nicholò di Francesco e Fratelli da Firenze deono avere in dì xiiij di maggio prossimo fior. quatrociento d., i quali gli promettemo a dì viiij di Febraio per Piero del Pucci, chatalano; posto adietro in questo ac. 82 Piero d'dare fior. cccc, d. .

E deono avere in dì xviiij d'aghosto fior. cientocinquanta, s. sedici, d. otto a oro, i quali denari gl'inprometemo per Giovanozo Biliotti e chompagni, posto inanzi in questo ac. 99 Giovanozo de'dare.
fior. cl, s. xvj, d. viij, o.
550/16/8 ·

Page 92

Debit Nicholò di Francesco e Fratelli on May 16 for 400 fiorini, which we paid for him to Banducio Bonchonti; cash disbursement book B was credited on page 132 by Simone di Francescho.   fior. 400, d.   .

Debit Nicholò on August 30 for 150 fior., 16 soldi, 8 denari a oro, which we paid for him to Banducio Bonchonti; cash disbursement book B was credited on page 143 by Francescho Bartolomeo.
            fior. 150, s. 16, d. 8.
            550/16/8

Page 92

Credit Nicholò di Francesco e Fratelli of Florence on May 14 for 400 fiorini, which were promised to him by us through Piero del Pucci, *chatalano;* Piero del Pucci is debited on page 82.
            fior. 400, d.   .

Credit Nicholò on August 19 for 150 fior., 16 soldi, 8 denari a oro, which was promised to him by us through Giovanozo Biliotti; Giovanozo is debited on page 99.
            fior. 150, s. 16, d. 8
            550/16/8

The debit entries have a cross reference to the cashbook B, and the credit entries are cross-indexed with other ledger accounts.

The profit-and-loss accounts from the same ledger are shown in the following example [18]:

ac. cccxxviiijt: +MCCCLXXIII

Quì apresso iscriveremo dano faremo di merchatantie che Idio ne guardi: di ij po (ndi) di ciera, chomperò Franciescho di Bonachorso in Gienova per noi, in questo c. 342.   fior.   , s. vij, d. vj.

ac. cccxxx:

pro faciamo di merchantantie iscriveremo quì apreso, chè Idio ne mandi sanità e ghuadagno, Amen.
Pro di chuoia e zucharo venduto, chome a le merchatantie A ac. 174.
            fior. xij, s. xij.

Page 329   1383

Here will be entered, God forbid, losses incurred on merchandise: 2 loads of wax, which Franciescho di Bonchorso bought for us at Gena, as shown on page 342.   fior.   , s. 7, d. 6.

Page 330

Profits on merchandise will be entered here, God grant us health and profits, Amen.

For profits on leather and sugar sold, as on merchandise A, the account is on page 174.   fior. 12, s. 12.

Thus it is clear that the lateral accounts were introduced in the Datini ledgers by applying them first to debtors' and creditors' accounts. The other accounts were gradually added as the usefulness of the new device became apparent. The bookkeeping technique of the Datini ledgers is far superior to Paliano's *vacchetta*. The application of the lateral accounts brought out in bold relief the underlying double-entry principle of Florentine bookkeeping, and any inconsistencies that may have existed were readily ironed out. By 1386, the ledgers at Pisa and Florence were on a complete lateral-account basis; by 1393, all the ledgers of all Datini's branches were on such a basis. At this time the complete double-entry system of bookkeeping was in general use throughout Tuscany.[19]

Before reaching a conclusion, something should be said about the remarkable balance-sheets (*bilanci*) of Florentine merchants. Ledgers during the fourteenth and fifteenth centuries were not usually balanced at any regular fiscal period; they covered any period from one to two or more years, and many ledgers were balanced only when completely filled and the open accounts were to be transferred to a new ledger. One notable exception was the Datini ledgers of the Avignon branch: they were regularly balanced at the end of every year and financial statements were prepared.

Because when the early writers on bookkeeping (Paciolo, Manzoni, Casanova, etc.) wrote about *inventari* and *bilanci*, they referred only to the procedure for closing accounts in a ledger and opening them in a new one, there is a common belief that true financial statements were nonexistent at this early period. This may be true of single ownerships, but it is not true of partnerships.[20] The *compagnie* of Florence, as has already been said, had developed the partnership contract to a high degree of perfection, and this entailed an equal development of partnership accounting, along with the financial statements necessary to show partners' interests.

The construction of these statements varied. The usual procedure seems to have been somewhat as follows: a *bilancio* (balance-sheet) was constructed from *inventari* (inventories) of all the assets and liabilities, drawn up at the end of the fiscal period, and the determination and division of profits and losses were based upon this *bilancio*.

These operations were called *saldamento della ragione*, i.e., the closing of the fiscal period.

A typical example of the *bilanci* used by Datini's Avignon branch is the one for the fiscal year of 1367–1368. In the Middle Ages, partnership capital accounts were usually kept in a separate secret account book.

The *bilancio* here reproduced is taken from secret red book 139 of the Avignon branch.[21]

Conti e Saldamento del Libro rosso segreto N. 139
  del Fondaco di Avignone

C. 7
Apresso faremo memoria del saldamento d'una noſtra ragione, la quale chominciò dì xxv d'ottobre anno MCCCLXVIJ, *di settenbre anno* MCCCLXVIIJ.

Trovamoci dì xvij di settenbre anno MCCCLXVIIJ *in Merchatantie e Masserizie nelle noſtre botteghe, chom'apare per lo quaderno di ragionamento rechate in soma fiorini tremilaciento quarantuno, s. ventitre, d. quattro.*

fior. mmmcxlj, *s.* xxiij, *d.* iiij

Trovamoci a dovere avere da più persone chom'apare a detto quaderno, i quali sono scritti al memoriale B e a libro grande giallo A, fiorini semila cinquecviento diciotto, s. ventitre, d. quattro. fior. $\frac{M}{vi}$dxviij, *s.* xxiij, *d.* iiij

Somma in tutto merchatantia, maserizie e chi de'dare fiorini novemila seciento sesanta, soldi ventidue, d. otto.   fior. $\frac{M}{viiij}$dclx, *s.* xxij, *d.* 8.

Trovamo dovere dare a più persone cho'apare per lo detto quaderno chontando in detta somma i due conpangni, cioè Franceschio e Toro che sono scritti nella carta sette qui adietro, montano in tutto fiorini settemila ottociento trentotto, s. diciotto, d. nove.   fior. vijdcccxxxviij, *s.* xviij, *d.* viiij.

Acci d'avanzo fatto a queſta ragione che cominciò a dì xxv d'ottobre anno MCCCLXVIJ *insino dì xvij di settenbre anno* MCCCLXVIIJ, *che sono x mesi, xxij dì, fior. mille ottociento ventidue, s. tre, d. undici.*

fior. mdcccxxij, *s.* iij, *d.* xj.

Il detto avanzo si parte in due parti, cioè l'una a Franciescho e l'altra a Toro:
Poſto che Franciescho deba avere in queſto a carte vj per la metà di detto avanzo fior. novecientoundici, s. due.   fior. dccccxj, *s.* ij

Poſto che Toro debba avere in queſto a carte vj per la metà di detto avanzo fior. noveciento undici, s. uno, d. undici.   fior. dccccxj, *s.* j, *d.* xj.

Accounts and closings of the secret red book No. 139 of the Avignon branch

Page 7
Below will be entered the closing of a fiscal period, which began October 25, 1367, and ended September 1368.
On September 27, 1368, we have in our ſtores merchandise, furniture, and fixtures amounting to 3141 fiorini, 23 soldi, and 4 denari, as shown in the account book.   fior. 3141, s. 23, d. 4.
Accounts receivable, as shown in the memorandum book B and in the yellow ledger A, amount to 6518 fiorini, 23 soldi, and 4 denari.

fior. 6518, s. 23, d. 4.

Total of merchandise, fixtures, and receivables amount to 9660 fiorini, 22 soldi, and 8 denari.   fior. 9660, s. 22, d. 8.

28

Total liabilities, as per ledger, including in said sum the capital of the two partners, i.e., Franciescho and Toro, taken from page 7 of this ledger, amount to 7838 fiorini, 18 soldi, and 9 denari.   fior. 7838, s. 18, d. 9.

The profit for the fiscal period, October 25, 1367, to September 17, 1368, the length of which is 10 months 22 days, amounts to 1822 fiorini, 3 soldi, and 11 denari.   fior. 1822, s. 3, d. 11.

This profit is divided into two parts, i.e., one to Franciescho and one to Toro:

Credit Franciescho, on page 6, for his half of the profit, amounting to 911 fiorini and 2 soldi.   fior. 911, s. 2.

Credit Toro on page 6, for his half of the profit, amounting to 911 fiorini, 1 soldo, and 11 denari.   fior. 911, s. 1, denari 11.

In a modernized form, the *bilancio* would appear somewhat as follows:

	Fiorini	Soldi	Denari
Merchandise and other assets in stores on September 27, 1368.	3,141	23	4
Accounts receivable.	6,518	23	4
Total assets	9,660	22	8
Total liabilities, including the capital accounts of the two partners, Franciescho and Toro.	7,838	18	9
Net profit for the fiscal period	1,822	3	11
The net profit is divided equally among the two partners:			
Franciescho 1/2 of profits	911	2	
Toro 1/2 of profits	911	1	11
Total profit distributed	1,822	3	11

The construction of the *bilancio* is obvious. The different totals making up the statement were gathered by means of inventories from the numerous secondary books used by these medieval bookkeepers. These totals were then handed to the partners, who drew up a *bilancio* and placed it in the partners' secret book. The net profits were determined by means of this *bilancio*, as seen in the example, by deducting from the total assets the total liabilities, including capital accounts. No separate profit-and-loss statement was used. The total net profit, as determined by this method, should agree with the total of the general profit account in the ledger.[22]

The Florentines, in conclusion, had developed, independently of Venice or Genoa, an efficient bookkeeping system that was based fundamentally on double entry, departing from it principally in the form of the account. When lateral accounts were introduced from Venice in the 1380's, no other fundamental changes were made in the bookkeeping technique, which gives evidence of the basic likeness of the two systems.

NOTES

[1] Edgcumbe, Staley. *The Guilds of Florence* (London, 1906), chap. 6, p. 185.

[2] Ceccherelli. Op. cit., chap. 2.
Edler, Florence. *Glossary of Medieval Terms of Business* (Cambridge, Medieval Academy of America, 1931), appendix 1, "Medici Partnerships," p. 335.

[3] Ceccherelli. Op. cit., chap. 3, p. 13.

[4] Ibid., Chap. 3, p. 14.

[5] Ibid., Chap. 3, p. 20.
Corsani. Op. cit., chap. 2, pp.44–46.

[6] As shown by Corsani (chap. 2, p. 57), types of books kept by Florentine merchants were:
  a. *Libri segreti* or *rivedimenti di conti*, private ledger holding partners' accounts.
  b. *Quaderni di ragionamento o di ragione*, where all *inventari* were entered.
  c. *Libri delle possessioni*, where all fixed assets were entered.
  d. *Quaderno di digrosso di debitori e creditori* or *stratti ed estratti*. All summaries of different books necessary for the drawing up of the *bilancio* were in this book.
  e. *Quaderni o quadernucci di ricordanze*. Transactions were gathered here daily preparatory to being entered into the ledger.
  f. *Memoriali* and *giornali*. Served the same purpose as the *quaderno di ricordanze*, and also the purposes of a cashbook.
  g. *Libro grande* or *campione*, a ledger; has an index (*stratto o alfabeto*).
  h. *Libri di entrata e uscita*, a cashbook; payments and receipts were kept distinctly apart: receipts entered in first half of book, disbursements in the last half. Any cash short and over was closed into profit and loss (*avanzi o disavanzi di cassa*).
  i. *Cassette piccole* and *cassa grande*, the first being petty cashbooks, the second the general cashbook.
  j. *Quaderni di cassa*, where accounts were kept of who *doveva dare o avere di denari contanti*, i.e., an A/R and A/P ledger.
  k. *Libri o quaderni di balle*, a merchandise book recording all merchandise received and shipped.
  l. *Libro delle lettere*, where all business letters were kept.
  m. *Spese di case*, book for domestic expenses, which was totaled at irregular intervals and entered into the cashbook.

[7] Quoting from Ceccherelli, chap. 3, p. 18: "Nevertheless, the distinction in partnerships between principal and secondary books appears clear even at that date. Naturally, when one applies methods of account based on a yet imperfect and incomplete theory, it is always necessary to use many auxiliary books. This is true of all ancient bookkeeping, not excepting the system used at Florence, which made use of auxiliary books. These books are of no particular interest, because their purpose was to gather and describe transactions which were later entered in the principal books."

[8] The lira was fictitious in that it was not a money of circulation, but was originally the coinage pound of metal. With the debasement of the coins of circulation, the term "*libbre*" came to signify 20 shillings, or 240 pence of the money of circulation; hence it was a collective, rather than a fictitious, unit. Only when debasement had carried the weight of its divisions down to such small size did it become a coin of circulation.

[9] Corsani. Op. cit., chap. 2, pp. 37–38.

   Ceccherelli. Op. cit., chap. 3, p. 20.

[10] Ceccherelli, chap. 3, p. 21, says that the account books of this early period ". . . generally open with a balance account containing all the debits and credits of the company. On the debit side are entered all debits, with cross-reference numbers to their corresponding credits and, vice versa, on the credit side are entered all the credits, with cross-reference numbers to their corresponding debits.

   "But, for every debit and credit mentioned in the initial balance account, individual accounts are opened in the same ledger, all with cross-references to it."

[11] Ceccherelli, Op. cit., chap. 3, p. 22.

[12] Ibid. Chap. 3, p. 34.

[13] Corsani. Op. cit., chap. 3, p. 67.

[14] Raymond De Roover states a different opinion in his article, "La Formation et l'Expansion de la Comptabilité à Partie Double," published in May, 1937. He maintains that the accounts are not of the vertical type and that each account is divided into two parts: the debits being placed in the first half of the ledger and the credits in the second half. In closing an account, it would be necessary to add the debits and credits, which appear in different sections of the ledger, transferring the lesser of the two to the page of the larger sum, in order to determine the difference. This does not seem to be the general rule.

   The examples quoted in the text are two vertical accounts, each of them complete in itself, not split into two parts and entered in different sections of the ledger. They consist of both a payable and a receivable account opened to the same party, because both types of transactions occur. Naturally, to determine the net amount due, the smaller one has to be deducted from the larger.

   However, there is one case supporting De Roover's contention; it occurs in the Datini's ledger of 1367 and is quoted by Enrico Bensa in his book, *Francesco di Marco da Prato* (p. 409).

   Though it is conceivable that accounts were split occasionally, especially in the case of very active accounts, it nevertheless seems illogical to suppose that such a practice was in general use among the Florentines. The existing available material indicates that more general use was made of vertical accounts than of split accounts.

[15] Corsani. Op. cit., chap. 3, p. 81.

[16] Ibid. Chap. 3, p. 135.

[17] Ibid. Chap. 3, p. 83.

[18] Abstracted from Corsani, chap. 3, p. 84.

[19] Corsani. Op. cit., chap. 3, p. 91.

[20] Ibid. Chap. 4, p. 142. Corsani quotes Ceccherelli's conclusion on Florentine balance-sheets: ". . . that the use of the balance-sheet was general in all medieval Florentine partnerships, correctly compiled, taken from the regular account books, and completed with results of a final general inventory; furthermore, it was an autonomous document destined to serve as a basis of partnership accounting, both of which received their rationale in the partners' contractual relationships."

[21] Ibid. Chap. 4, p. 167.

   Another type of *bilancio* is given in part I, chapter 4, under the title, " Florentine Industrial Accounting."

[22] Ibid. Chap. 4, p. 156.

Chapter III

VENICE

ENICE was truly the foremost commercial city of the Renaissance, her greatness arising from her vast commercial empire in the East and her natural advantages as a port. The clash of the Eastern and Western civilizations brought Venice into being and was the principal factor in her whole future development. She was the active center of trade between the East and the West and her profits were enormous, though later the shifting of the trade route to the Atlantic dried up her lucrative sources of income, and her decline and final doom were inevitable.

It was natural that Venice should have developed the famous Venetian method of double entry. Her supremacy in commerce is responsible for the spread of the system to other parts of Italy during the fourteenth and fifteenth centuries, and in the sixteenth century, with the help of Venetian writers, throughout Europe.

Specimens of the most ancient Venetian account books that have a bearing on the origin of double entry will be shown in this chapter. The exposition of the system by later Venetian writers will be reserved for subsequent chapters.

The earliest Venetian double-entry books that have come to light so far date from the year 1406, considerably later than those of Genoa and Florence. It should not be inferred, however, that double entry originated any later at Venice than at other commercial centers of Italy. The earliest Venetian double-entry records showed a high degree of development. Among these records appears the first true journal encountered in Renaissance bookkeeping; previous to this, only the ledger, supplemented by numerous memorandum books, had been used. Such a system, which included the true application of the principle of double entry, lateral accounts, and a journal, must have taken a long time to evolve. It was recognized as the foremost system of double entry of its time.

The records which will be examined are three:

1. The ledger of the possessions of the rebels of Padua.
2. Soranzo Brothers' ledger.
3. Ledgers and journals of Andrea Barbarigo.

The ledger of the possessions of the rebels of Padua, *Quaderno delle possessioni dei ribelli di Padua*, is the most ancient Venetian government ledger in existence. It is written on parchment of sheepskin, with the accounts divided laterally and the two parts, debit and credit, placed on the same page.

Some of its accounts date back to 1406. Venice had annexed Padua to its territory the year before (1405), and the ledger records all the possessions of the citizens of Padua who opposed its rule. There are many entries indicating confiscation and sale of rebel property. An example from the year 1417 is here shown: [1]

Carte xj *tergo*   MCCCCXVIJ

Ser Marcho da Ponte de Venizia die   *Ser Marcho controscritto . . . die*
dar per uno quarto de la gastaldia de   *aver . . .*
Arquà, messo debbe aver in questo car.
II.   *lib.* $\overline{\text{M}}$
                                 iiij

Page 11 verso

1417

Debit Ser Marcho da Ponte de Venizia   Credit Ser Marcho as per contra . . .
for one fourth of cost for the garrison
of Arquà, which is credited on page 2.
               libbre 4,000

The credit of this entry is found on the same page, as follows:

Ser Marcho da Ponte de Venizia die   *Ser Marcho da Ponte de Venizia die*
dar . . .   *aver . . .*
                                      E a dì dito (dui aprile 1417) per un suo
                                      quarto de la gastaldia de Arquà, messo
                                      debia dar in questo car, II.   *lib.* $\overline{\text{M}}$
                                                              iiij

Debit Ser Marcho da Ponte de Veni-   Credit Ser Marcho da Ponte de Venizia . . .   zia . . .
                                      on the said date (April 2, 1417) for his
                                      1/4 of the cost of garrison de Arquà,
                                      which is debited on page 2. libbre 4,000

This transaction is cross-indexed with two accounts made out to the same person. All other transactions involving cash are recorded only in the account of the person affected, because there is no cash account in the ledger. The ledger is not self-balancing. This is a partial application of double entry.

    The next record is a ledger of a mercantile firm belonging to the Soranzo Brothers, *Fraterna di ser Donado, Jachomo, Piero, e Lorenzo Soranzo, fo de miser Vetor.* It contains 168 pages and its transactions range from August, 1406, to March, 1434. It began with a *bilancio* taken from an old ledger (*libro vecchio*

33

real), meaning that the open accounts of the old ledger were transferred to the new ledger by means of a balance account. The first entries of such a *bilancio* are here set forth: [2]

MCCCCVJ

Debitori e chreditori tratti del l'eſtratto fato per ser Jachomo Boltremo de dar per ser Donado Soranzo proprio fin dì 19 Agoſto, par in quello k76, in queſto k3,   lb. cij, s. v, d. vj.

et per ser Fantin Morexini, par in quella a k. 76, in queſto k. 4.

*   lib.   , s. j, d. viij, p. 16.*

et per noſtre amede le munege, par in quello a k. 76, in queſto a k. 4.

*   lib. j.*

MCCCCVJ

Debitori e chreditori tratti del l'eſtratto fato per ser Jachomo Boltremo de aver per la chamera da impreſtidi, par in quello k. 76,78, in queſto k. 2u

*   lib. cxxvj, s. v, d. iiij, p. 27.*

et per ser Bernardo Marioni par in quello a k. 76 in queſto k. 2.

*   lb.   , s. ij.*

et per Commissaria ser Piero Benedeto e compagni, par in quello a k. 76, in queſto k. 2.

*   lb. lxx, s. vij, d. ij, p. 1.*

1406

Debit on Auguſt 19 debtors and creditors extracted from the *bilancio*, on page 76 of that ledger, drawn up for Jachomo Boltremo, and credit in this ledger, on page 3, Ser Donado Soranzo   lb. 102, s. 5, d. 6.

and credit ser Fantin Morexini, in that ledger page 76, in this ledger page 4.   lib.   , s. 1, d. 8, p. 16.

and credit our friends the nuns, in that ledger page 76, in this ledger page 4.

      lib. 1

1406

Credit debtors and creditors extracted from the bilancio, on pages 75 and 78 of that ledger, drawn up for Jachomo Boltremo, and debit the office of public loans, in this ledger on page 2.

      lib. 126, s.   , d. 3, p. 27.

and debit ser Bernardo Marioni, in that ledger on page 76, in this ledger on page 2.   lib.   , s. 2.

and debit ser Piero Benedeto e compagni for commissions, in that ledger on page 76, in this ledger on page 2.   lib. 70, s. 7, d. 2, p. 1.

The principle of double entry is correctly applied; the accounts are divided laterally and all transactions are cross-indexed.

Of much more importance are the bookkeeping records of the Barbarigo family. Here is encountered, for the firſt time, a perfectly coördinated syſtem of journal and ledger, which was one of the chief reasons for the superiority of the Venetian method. The Barbarigo records include journals and ledgers which cover, almoſt without interruption, the period from 1431 to 1582. During the earlier years the records were chiefly concerned with commercial ventures, and in later years with the possessions of the Barbarigo family. The first journal, belonging to Andrea Barbarigo, begins with the following entries: [3]

> *In Christi nomine in MCCCCXXX a dì 2 zenaro in Venexia.*
>
> 18 / 7   *Per cassa de constanti A ser Francesco Balbi e fradelli contadi da ser Nicholò de Bernardo e fradelli e ser Matio e ser Zan de garzoni per nome de ser Armano per resto de zaferan duc 4, g. 3, p. 16 val.*
> *lb. , s. viij, d. iij, p. 16.*
>
> *1430 a dì 8 zenaro*
>
> 5 / 14   *Per ser Nofrio decalzi de Lucha A ser Francesco Balbi e fradelli per le bancho i de contar per mi.*   *lb. iij, s , d , p. 0.*
>
> *1430 a dì 22 zenaro*
>
> 18 / 18   *Per spexe per mio conto A cassa ch'i o spexo per andar a Ferrara duc. 3 1/2*   *lb. , s. vij, d. 0, p. 0.*
> 18 / 18   *Per spexe per mio conto A cassa per uno libro e per questo ziornal duc. 2.*   *lb. , s. iiij, d. 0, p. 0.*

In the year of our Lord, January 2, 1430, Venice.

18 / 7   Debit cash; credit ser Francesco Balbi and brothers, farmhands for ser Nicholò de Bernardo and brothers, and ser Matio and ser Zan de Garzoni, in the name of ser Armano, for the remainder of saffron valued at 4 ducati, 3 grossi, 16 piccioli.   lib. , s. 8, d. 3, p. 16.

January 8, 1430

5 / 14   Debit ser Nofrio Decalzi de Lucha; credit ser Francesco Balbi and brothers for the money due me.   lib. 3, s. , d. , p. 0.

January 22, 1430

18 / 18   Debit personal expenses; credit cash for traveling expenses to Ferrara, 3 1/2 duc.   lib. , s. 7, d. 0, p. 0.
18 / 18   Debit personal expenses; credit cash for the purchase of ledger and journal, 2 duc.   lib. , s. 4, d. 0, p. 0.

These entries are sufficient to illustrate the nature of the journal used. The debit and credit of each entry are not separated, but combined in one paragraph with all the details of the transaction. The debit and credit are distinguished from one another by the use of the prepositions *per* and *A*. *Per* stands for debit and *A* for credit. [4] The money values are placed at the end of the transaction on the right-hand side of the page, forming a crude money column. The fractions on the left-hand side of the page are the cross-reference numbers of the ledger accounts, the numerator being the ledger folio of the debit entry and the denominator the ledger folio of the credit entry.

The index system undergoes, therefore, one notable change: The ledger, as will be seen, is cross-indexed between accounts in exactly the same fashion as the older ledgers, but the journal is now introduced and all its entries are cross-indexed, by means of fractions, with the ledger accounts. The latter, though, have no cross-reference numbers referring to the journal. The only way to trace a ledger entry to the journal is by means of the date.

The ledger itself begins with a balance account, which serves as the medium for the transfer of open accounts from a previous ledger. The first few entries are quoted below:[5]

MCCCCXXX

Debitori et creditori trati dal libro biancho picholo A deno dar a dì 2 zenaro per Andrea Barbarigo che fui de Messer Nicholò chome apar in quelle a k. 2. lb. xx,s. , d. , p. o.
A dì 2 zenaro per provizion che o trate de mercantie k. 2.
lb. lij, s. , d. , p. o.

MCCCCXXX

Debitore et creditori controscritti deno aver a dì 2 zenaro per ser Piero Soranzo fo de ser Antonio apar in questo k. 7.
lb. , s. xiij, d. x, p. o.
A dì 2 zenaro per ser Stefano Fin vianza el vianza de la tana k. 8.
lb. , s. j, d. ij, p. 28.

1430

Debit on January 2 debtors and creditors taken from page 2 of the small white book A, and credit Andrea Barbarigo of the late Meser Nicholò.
lib. 20, s. , d. , p. o.
On January 2, for provisions I have taken from merchandise; credit the latter on page 2.
lib. 52, s. , d. , p. o.

1430

Credit on January 2 debtors and creditors as per contra, and debit on page 7 ser Piero Soranzo, son of the late ser Antonio.
lib. , s. 13, d. 10, p. o.
On January 2, debit on page 8 ser Stefano Fin, who is traveling to Tana. lib. , s. 1, d. 2, p. 28.

The journal and ledger of Andrea Barbarigo mark one of the high points in the evolution of double entry. The two records have now become essential to each other and together form a unified whole, with the cross-index system and the date serving as the coördinators. The principle of double entry is correctly applied throughout. This system, vastly superior to all others, was applied for centuries, not only in Venice and in all other Italian regions, but under the name of the Venetian method or Italian method, in all civilized countries.

CONCLUSION

With Venice ends what may be conveniently termed the origins of double entry. No one particular locality may lay exclusive claim to being the birthplace of the system. The causes of its appearance and of its development are to be found and explained only in that burst of intellectual, artistic, and commercial activity which characterized the Italy of the Communes and of the Renaissance.

Double entry was not conceived as a whole, but came about gradually, imperceptibly — the result of efforts of generations of merchants who unwittingly contributed to its origin and evolution by modifying their crude systems of bookkeeping to meet the exigencies of a fast growing foreign trade.

The records which have so far come to light do not uncover the very beginnings of double entry. The Venetian records reveal the system in full maturity. The Massari ledgers of Genoa are also drawn up on a true double-entry basis. In the Florentine ledgers, one may trace the introduction of lateral accounts, but the preëxisting system, as shown in these records, was essentially double entry in character.

How much Venice contributed to the origin of this system is not known. But one thing is certain, that whatever the origin of double entry, Venice used and developed it, perfected it, and made it her own, and it was under the name of the Venetian method that it became known the world over.

NOTES

[1] Besta. Op. cit., vol. 3, p. 302.
[2] Ibid. Vol. 3, bk. 9, chap. 9, art. 3.
[3] Ibid.
[4] The literal translation of *Per* and *A* would be "for" and "to." However, *Per* and *A* indicate debtor and creditor, and it is therefore best to translate them as debit and credit.
[5] Besta. Op. cit., vol. 3, bk. 9, chap. 9, art. 3.

Chapter IV

FLORENTINE INDUSTRIAL ACCOUNTING[1]

LORENCE was preëminently an industrial city. From the twelth century she was famous for her silk and wool industries. Her international banking business began as an adjunct to her industries; industrialists found it profitable to establish a banking, or rather an exchange, business to facilitate the disposal of their products throughout Europe. Banking soon outgrew the phase in which it received its first impetus, but even at its highest development many banks retained their industrial business.

The origin and development of industrial cost accounting in Florence owes much to the city's guild system. All Florentine industries were incorporated into separate guilds and each guild jealously guarded its trade secrets, privileges, and rights against the encroachments, both in Florence and abroad, of all outsiders. To further enforce this protection, the Florentine Republic enacted laws, supported by guild by-laws, absolutely forbidding the emigration of skilled workers and the export of material and objects belonging to the guilds.

The division of industries into guilds was carried further within the guild itself. The skilled workmen of a guild were divided into trade associations, each association representing skilled artisans of a process in the manufacturing sequences of an industry. No workman, however skilled, was allowed to practise his trade if he was not a member of the guild and of the trade association within the guild.

The manufacture of wool was the leading industry of Florence, and its guild was among the most important. Early in its history, the Calimala guild was established and its business was the redressing and finishing of foreign-woven woolen cloth. The wool guild, on the other hand, was devoted to the manufacture of domestic woolen cloth. The two guilds kept strictly within their chosen fields.

Staley, on page 149 of his book, *The Guilds of Florence*, says that among the trade associations subordinated to the Guild of Wool Merchants were:

Tosatori and cimatori	Shearers
Lavatori	Washers
Scompatori	Sorters
Cardatori and scardassieri	Carders
Filatori and filatore	Spinners — male and female
Tessitori	Weavers

38

Folloni	Fullers
Tintori	Dyers
Filatrice	Winders
Stamaiuoli	Master-spinners
Battilani	Carding-machine oilers
Lanini	Special workers
Pettinatori	Combers
Vergheggiatori and battitori	Beaters
Pettinagnoli	Comb makers
Conciatori	Curriers

"The dyers of Florence," says Staley on page 151, "formed a considerable and numerous element in the population." They seem to have been divided into three classes:

1. Dyers of foreign cloth for the Calimala guild;
2. Dyers of native cloth for the wool guild; and
3. Dyers of silk for the silk guild.

All were dependent upon the Calimala for the supply of dyes, mordants, and all other ingredients of their trade. Each dyer paid the sum of 310 gold florins to the treasurer of the guild, by way of guarantee or bond that he purposed to execute his calling in good faith, and in return received official permission to carry on the industry. Each dye-house and all its contents, together with samples of dyed goods, were required to be prepared annually for a thorough inspection by the officials of the guild.

While the dyers were not permitted to incorporate into a separate *arte*, or guild, they were allowed to associate, in families and other groups, in the pursuit of any special operations of the craft. All such companies were subordinated to the wool guild, with respect to their political and social status, the only exception being made in the case of certain foreign dyers employed by the silk guild, who did not come under the authority of the wool guild.

It is easy to see how the Florentine bookkeeping system had to adapt itself to the guild system and keep separate records for the costs of each process of manufacture, because it involved engaging workmen belonging to different trade associations who did not necessarily perform the work on the premises, but often took it to their own establishments. This segregation of costs finally resulted in the Florentine industrial bookkeeping system. It is but a crude beginning, since it determines only the prime costs of goods manufactured, but it is nevertheless significant because the origin of cost accounting has been placed by some at the time of the Industrial Revolution.

Florentine industries were faced with bookkeeping problems quite different from those encountered in mercantile businesses; they had to develop special records to keep track of costs of goods manufactured, and in the fourteenth century a cost technique was developed which holds, as far as it is known, the origins of industrial cost accounting.

Despite the numerous industries in Florence at the beginning of the fourteenth century, complete bookkeeping records of the period are rare. Those of Del Bene's firm (cost records of *Del Bene dell'arta della Lana*, Del Bene of the Guild of Woolen Manufacturers, 1368), reaching as far back as 1318, are an exception. Costs at first were entered in the principal account books of this firm in the same manner that expenses were entered in mercantile books, but soon the necessity for determining the costs of products manufactured and their profits made itself felt. In response to this need, there gradually appeared, through a natural process of separation, two sets of books: one dealing with the mercantile phase, and the other dealing with the industrial phase of the business. This was near the middle of the fourteenth century.

To determine the cost of products manufactured, the method devised was to keep as many separate books as there were important elements entering into the total cost of goods produced. In Del Bene's wool industry there were three important cost records:

1. *Libri delle lane*,
     To record the cost price of raw wool purchased;
2. *Libri dei lavoranti* and
3. *Libri dei tintori*,
     To record all the labor expenses incurred in the manufacture and dyeing of woolen cloth, i.e., the direct labor costs of goods produced.

These three books together gave the total prime cost of goods produced. Three abstracts, one from each of the cost books of the Del Bene firm, illustrate typical transactions.

1. *Libro delle Lane* (Book of raw wool purchased):
     The transactions are entered here in the form of a bill. Each entry bears the date of purchase, the name of the seller, the place of purchase, the mark (in the nature of a trade-mark) indicating the quality of the wool, and finally the price:

VI *Balle di lama lunga d'Inghilterra de la marca segn ÷ M.A. ÷ comprammo da Lande d'Antonio degli albizi il dì* I *di settembre fior.* MMMCCCCXXXXVII, *s.* XL

Tara	*s.* CLVI
Tara per fracido	*s.* XX
Tara per bigio	*s.* X

Resta necta fiorini MMMCCLM, *s.* XL

Bought on September 1 from Land od'Antonio degli albizi 6 bales of long staple English wool of the trade mark ÷ M.A. ÷ for 3447 fiorini, 40 soldi

Tare	s. 156
Tare for humidity	s. 20
Tare for gray	s. 10

Net amount — fiorini 3,750, s. 40

2. *Libre dai Lavoranti* (Laborers wage book):

Here are recorded all labor expenses necessary to manufacture a certain quantity and quality of woolen cloth. The entries are made in the following way:

MCCCLXVIII
Tintilani Azurini arcistrofinissimi

chosto di netare biancho e tinta	aff.
chosto di vergheggiare bianco	aff.
chosto di schamatore tinta	aff.

Pettinare

Francesco e Compagni p. 47 ÷ di lama 929 olio p. v. il quarto p. pennecchiare.

Schardassare

Francesco e Compagni p. 93 ÷ di lama.
p. nettare.
p. pettini e chardi.

Soma aff. XXXVIII, *s.* I, *d.* VIII

1368
Extra fine blue (wool)

Cost for washing white and colored wool	aff.
Cost for beating white wool	aff.
Cost for beating colored wool	aff.

Combing

Francesco and Compagni, for 47 ÷ wool, 929 quarts of oil at 5 per quart.
For arranging wool on distaffs

Wool carding

Francesco and Compagni, p. 93 ÷ wool
For washing
For combs and cards

Total fiorini 38, soldi 1, denari 8.

3. *Libre dei Tintori* (Dyers wage book):

This is similar to the book of the *laboranti*, except that costs here are not kept on the basis of quantity of cloth, but rather are kept in accounts opened for each individual *tintore* (dyer). Each account takes care of labor costs for dyeing incurred by one laborer:

Ugolino di Marcho, tintore di grado

1 Biancho 57	dì VIII di Maggio	chupo	aff. XVI, s. IIII
1 Biancho	dì —— di Giugno	chupo	aff. XVI, s. IIII
1 Sbiadito 59	dì —— di Luglio	azurino	aff. XI, s. X

Soma aff. XLIII s. XVIII

Ugolino di Marcho, skilled dyer

1 White 57	May 8	black	aff. 16, s. 4
1 White	June 8	black	aff. 16, s. 4
1 Pale blue	July 8	light blue	aff. 11, s. 10

Total fiorini 43, s. 18.

These three books, therefore, when totaled and combined, furnished the manufacturer with the prime costs of woolen cloth produced.

The sales were recorded in two different books:

1. *Memoriali di vendita*

A record of all goods sent out on consignment to be sold on a commission basis.

2. *Libri di vendita*

Sales books recording actual sales.

An example of each will be given below.

1. *Memoriali di Vendita* (Consignment memorandum book):

The notations in this memorandum book were limited to the recording of the consignment of cloth shipped, the date, name, and place:

MCCCLXVII

Memoria che a dì 1 giugno MCCCLXVIII mandammo per Neri d'Astiano vetturale a Stoldo di Lapo a Napoli che ci vendesse una balla panni.

Una balla panni

XIII	*sbiadito*	13
XIII	*celestino*	22
XIII	*violetto*	14
XIII	*sambucato*	13
VI	*turchino*	20

42

Una balla panni

VI	turchino	20
XIII	scharlatto	14
XIIII	verdebruno	14
XIII	bruno	19
XIII	cilestro	22

1367

Memo: June 1, 1368, we shipped by Neri d'Aſtiano to Stoldo di Lapo at Naples a bale of cloths to be sold for us.

One bale of cloths

XIII	pale blue	13
XIII	blue	22
XIII	violet	14
XIII	cream	13
VI	dark blue	20

One bale of cloths

VI	dark blue	20
XIII	red (vermilion)	14
XIIII	dark green	14
XIII	brown	19
XIII	blue	22

2. *Libro di Vendita* (Sales book):

All details of actual sales are entered in this book:

Manetto di Donolo da Taranto de dare a dì 1 Maggio MCCCLXVI p. i sottoscritti panni vendè Jachopo a Trani a termine in su la fiera di san Martino a Barletta de' sodetti denari ci debe dare Jachopo e Piero del Botte a San Martino.

I	Chupo	146	h. VI	b. II	aff. XXXIII	s. VIII	d. XI
÷	Violetto	9	VI	b. II	aff. XXXVIII	s. VIII	d.
÷	Mischio	22	XII	b. II	aff. LXVIIII	s. III	d. VIIII
÷	Azurino	20	VI	b. II	aff. XXXVIII	s. VIII	d. I
	Chupo	36	VI	b. II	aff. XXXII	s. XII	d. VI
÷	Romanesco	30	VI	b. II	aff. XLII	s. XVI	d.
	Bianco	24	VI		aff. XXXII	s. XII	d.
	Monachino	28	XIII	II	aff. LXXIII	s. XI	d. VI
	Bruschino	27	XIII	II	aff. LXVII	s. XII	d. VI

Soma aff. CCCCXLV *s.* VII *d.* X

De dare per porto a ragione di V *per centinaio* aff. XXII *s.* , *d.*
De dare per spese aragione di f. II *p. panno* aff. XXI *s.* , *d.*

Soma in tutto aff. CCCCLXXXVIII, *s.* VII, *d.* X

43

May 1, 1366, debit Manetto di Donolo da Taranto for cloths listed below which were sold to him by Jachopo a Trani on time at the San Martino fair at Barletta, which sum Jachopo e Piero del Botte shall pay us at San Martino at maturity of obligation.

I	black	146	h. VI	b. II	aff. 33	s. 8	d. 11
÷	violet	9	VI	b. II	aff. 38	s. 8	d.
÷	mixture	22	XII	b. II	aff. 69	s. 3	d. 9
÷	light blue	20	VI	b. II	aff. 38	s. 8	d. 1
	black	36	VI	b. II	aff. 32	s. 12	d. 6
÷	claret-red	30	VI	b. II	aff. 42	s. 16	d.
	white	24	VI	b. II	aff. 32	s. 12	d.
	monkish-grey	28	XIII	II	aff. 73	s. 11	d. 6
	coffee color	27	XIII	II	aff. 67	s. 12	d. 6

Total aff. 445, s. 7, d. 10

Debit for transportation charges 5% aff. 22, s.   , d.
Debit for expenses fior. 2 per cloth   aff. 21, s.   , d.

Total aff. 488, s. 7, d. 10

Thus it is seen that the two sets of books furnished the manufacturer with the prime costs of woolen cloth produced and with the sales of such cloth. To determine net profit, the manufacturer at certain intervals summarized all the secondary books, cost and otherwise, and entered the totals in the ledger. At this stage, industrial and mercantile operations of the business had been merged.

The manufacturing periods were divided in length according to the time necessary for the manufacture of a certain fixed quantity of cloth. All costs and sales were based on this quantity of cloth, and anything over and above this was deferred to the next period. A *bilancio*, from which the profits or losses were ascertained, was drawn up at the end of each period. Each manufacturing period was named *ragione*, and was distinguished from the others by a letter of the alphabet.

The *bilancio* is in approximately the same form as the one encountered in the Datini records discussed earlier. Total liabilities, including capital and deferred sales, are deducted from total assets, the resultant being the profit for the period. The assets and liabilities are given in detail, and their totals are then made the basis of the *bilancio*. The period set forth in the following pages is designated by "h" (*ragione segnata* "h").

ASSETS

MCCCLXIIII *addi 1 Marzo*
March 1, 1364

Chi dee dare a' libri per la ragione segnata "h"
Assets of fiscal period "h"

Gianzo degli strozzi e Lapo Ranzati	*a libro bianco nel* white book page			63	*aff.* 122	9
Francesco di Jacopo	"	"	"	62	*aff.* 290	
Francesco di Jacopo	"	"	"	70	71	15
Francesco di Piero Bone	"	"	"	70	29	18
Guglielmo di Ciardo	"	"	"	71	28	8
Marcho di Lorenzo	"	"	"	71	42	
Giovanni di Francesco	"	"	"	71	8	
Messer Gherardo Buondelmonti ed altri	"	"	"	71	79	
Bettino di Messer Bindaccio	"	"	"	74	316	15
M. Bene di Jacopo	"	"	"	75	377	6
Francesco di Jacopo	"	"	"	75	630	
Borgonone di Jacopo	"	"	"	76	3,530	17
Jacopo di Bonaccorso	*alla casas nel* cash book page			45	13	9
Lionardo di Bartolomeo	"	"	"	49	16	5
Piero di Gherardo	"	"	"	54	5	16
Giovanni d'Agnolo	"	"	"	71	8	5
Jacopo di Francesco	"	"	"	69	102	15
Jacopo di Neri Paganelli	"	"	"	70	24	11
Bisio Guasconi	"	"	"	71	8	5
Gherardo di Bartolo Filippi	"	"	"	73	514	12
Mona Pasquina	"	"	"	76	2	15
Gherardo di Francesco	"	"	"	77	10	15

Somma aff. $\overline{\text{m}}$ X.VI
$\overline{\text{VI}}$CCLV

ASSETS (continued)

Cienni di Monsierone	al quaderno cassa nel		79	aff.	14	10
	cash book page					
Mona Piera di Domenico	"	"	"	79	8	8
Mona Orsa	"	"	"	79	4	8
Bianco di Bonsi	"	"	"	79	182	9
M. Lazaro di M. Ricardo	"	"	"	79	87	17
Michele di Pruosio	"	"	"	79	2	6
Mofrio di Giovanni e Chompagni	"	"	"	79	110	6
Andrea di Agostino	"	"	"	79	5	15
Giovanni di Chatelino	"	"	"	79	135	15
Domenico di Filippi	"	"	"	79	35	12
Giovanni di Lenzo	"	"	"	79	6	9
Guglielmo di Liardo	"	"	"	79	192	8
Bartolomeo di Lapo Bombeni	"	"	"	79	121	
Francesco dal Pistoia	"	"	"	79	5	16
Pieri di Puccio	"	"	"	79	21	15
Chompiobino	"	"	"	79	7	11
Divetini	"	"	"	79	2	14
Nofrio di Lienni	"	"	"	79	1	9
Andrea di Chito	"	"	"	79	2	18
Nicholo di Lorenzo	"	"	"	79	7	4
Jacopo di Guarnelotto	"	"	"	79	1	5
Tomaso di Vanni	"	"	"	79	26	19
Carlo di Stroza	"	"	"	79	362	10
Mona Savia	"	"	"	79	2	18

Somma aff. MCCCLXII

ASSETS (continued)

Piero di Giovanni Stumetti	79	*aff.* 107	
Cardatori a cassa Teaslers, cash book	89	*aff.* 108	2
Al guadernuccio dei fogli in più carte e a più persone From small ledger of diverse accounts and persons		166	8
Al guaderno della Ricordanze h per la ragione I Memorandum book "h" for fiscal period I		66	12

Merchandise on hand and in process.	*Al guaderno delle lane in più persone* From raw wool book for diverse persons	1,392	
	Al libro dei lavoranti in più carte From laborers wage book	905	19
	Al libro dei filatori in più carte From spinners wage book	840	7
	Al libro dei tessitori in più carte From weavers wage book	660	10
	Al libro dei tintori in più carte From dyers wage book	51	
	Al libro dei tintori da più carte e da più persone From dyers wage book	224	16

Borgonne di Jacopo a libro vendite Sales book 14	442	
Un panno cupo del 47 ragioniamolo Black cloth No. 47 valued at	56	

$$\textit{Somma aff.} \quad \underset{\overline{V}}{m} \text{XXI} \quad \text{VIII}$$

*Somma delle Somme di chi dee dare come appare in questo
quaderno in dietro in due faccie in questa* — aff. 12638, 9.

*Somma delle somme di chi dee avere da noi come appare in
questo quaderno innanzi in una faccia e in venti
partite* — aff. 10856, 10.

*Somma che Dio ci ha conceduto di guadagno di panni
che abbiamo fatti in 12 mesi finita addì 1 marzo
MCCCLXIIII nella ragione segnata h.* — aff. 1781, 19.

Ponemmo questo guadagno a libro bianco a carte 43.

	Fiorini	soldi
Total assets as shown on the last three pages	12,638	9
Total liabilities as shown on the next page	10,856	10
Net profit which God saw fit to allow us for the past 12 months ended today March 1, 1364, for the fiscal period "h"	1,781	19

This profit is posted on page 43 of the White Book

LIABILITIES

MCCCLXIIII *addì 1 Marzo*
March 1, 1364

Chi dee avere a libri per la ragione segnata h.
Liabilities of fiscal year "h"

Giovanni Ormani	*Libro Bianco* 63	*aff.*	6		2
	White Book				
Partners' ⌈ *Jacopo di Francesco*	" "	53	2,273		8
capital ⟨ *Stoldo di Lapo Stoldi*	" "	53	1,689		6
accounts. ⌊ *Francesco di Jacopo*	" "	53	2,251		2
Frate Giovanni Guidotti	" "	61	290		
Riccardo di Piero	" "	69	1,055		
Tebalino de' Ricci e C.	" "	74	372	12	
Bartolomeo panciatichi	" "	74	79	15	
Piero Guicciardini	" "	74	216		6
Bartolomeo Cancellieri	*Libro Cassa* 5		5		5
	Cash Book				
Marco Bini	" "	55	26		7
Salveſtro e Marco pettinatori (combers)	" "	5	29		
Ciro Cirioni	" "	75	71	17	
Borgonone de Jacopo	" "	76	186	13	
Michele di Bartolo	" "	79	16	10	
Bartolomeo di Caroccio	" "	79	22		
Lapo di Stoldo	" "	79	14		2
Chirigoso di Michele	" "	19	4	15	
Vendite che abbiamo messo alla ragion nuova			2,054	11	
Sales deferred to the next period.[2]					
Stoldi di Capo Stoldi	*Libro Bianco* 52		12		10
	White Book				

Somma aff. 10856, 10

Posta queſta somma dietro a piè della somma di chi ci dee dare.
This sum is deducted on previous page from assets.

Thus ascertained, the profit for the period was entered into a special book (*libro bianco*), where it was distributed among the partners in accordance with their profit-and-loss ratios.

Libro Bianco a carte 43:

Memoria che a dì VI di dicembre ano MCCCLXV saldiamo la ragione di panni segnata h che facemo in 12 mesi chominciati in kal. di marzo ano MCCCLXIIII e finita in kal di marzo ano MCCCLXV troviamo che Dio ci ha choncieduto di guadagno aff. millestecento ottanta uno s. dicianove chome appare a uno quadernuccio di fogli segnato h il quale tenghiamo in questo libro   *aff. MDCCLXXXI s. XVIIII*

Ponemo a ragione di Jacopo di Francesco proprio deba avere in dì primo marzo ano MCCCLV innanzi nel 53 per la parte che gli tocca   C

                                       aff. $\overline{\text{IIII}}$XXXVIII s. X

Ponemo a ragione di Francesco di Jacopo proprio che deba avere in dì primo marzo MCCCLXV per la parte che gli tocca.   C

                                       aff. $\overline{\text{IIII}}$LII s. X

Ponemo a ragione di Stoldo di Lapo Stoldi proprio deba avere in dì primo marzo ano MCCCLXV per la parte che gli tocca.

                                     aff. DCCCLXXXX s. XVIIII

White Book at page 43:

	Fiorini	Soldi
On this day December 6, 1365, net profits for the 12-month fiscal period "h" ended on March 1, 1365 were [3]	1,781	19
Transfer to Jacopo di Francesco's account, on page 53, his share of the profits	438	10
Transfer to Francesco di Jacopo his share of profits	452	10
Transfer to Stoldo di Lapo Stoldi his share of profits	890	19
	1,781	19

NOTES

[1] Based on Ceccherelli. Op. cit., chap. 4, pp. 40–53.
[2] The cloth sold belongs to the next period and, therefore, these sales are deferred until the next period also, so that the profit calculation will show the true profit for the period in question.
[3] The calendar year began on March 1st.

PART II

THE LITERATURE OF ACCOUNTING

THE FIRST CYCLE
1458 - 1558

THE SECOND CYCLE
1559 - 1795

THE THIRD CYCLE
1796 TO DATE

Chapter V

THE FIRST CYCLE (1458 - 1558)

WRITERS on double entry did not appear until the system was well developed and widely used. Strangely enough, the first writers to treat the subject were not bookkeepers, or *quadernieri*, as they were called in various regions of Italy, but learned men, who wrote *summae*, touching on all fields of knowledge; to round out their treaties, they would include a few chapters on the merchants' art of keeping books. The *summa* began to appear just as Italy entered upon a period of political decadence. France, Germany, and Spain ravaged her with long wars, starting in 1495 with the invasion of the French king Charles VIII and ending in 1796 with Napoleon's Italian campaign.

During these three centuries the commercial and political supremacy of the Italian republics and principalities passed to the nations on the Atlantic Ocean and Central Europe. This was due to the encroachments of the Turks on the Eastern commercial empires of Venice and Genoa, to inherent weaknesses of the small Italian states, and to the discovery of new routes to India and China. The shifting of the flow of commerce from the Mediterranean to the Atlantic dried up the sources of Italy's wealth, and thereafter she was steadily pushed into the background until the greater part of the land was under foreign rule. The Renaissance movement, however, did not cease at the end of the fifteenth century, though unmistakable seeds of decay were undermining the political greatness of the Italian states; it continued unabated through the sixteenth century, producing such geniuses as Ariosto, Tasso, Machiavelli, Guicciardini, Michelangelo, and Leonardo da Vinci. In the great production of literary, artistic, and scientific works, bookkeeping also came in for its share of attention.

The pioneer writers on double entry are Cotrugli, Paciolo, and Cardano — not one of them a bookkeeper. Cotrugli, native of Dalmatia, was a judge at the court of Naples under King Alfonso (*auditore della Ruota napoletana*), and under the son, Ferdinand, he was ambassador to many princes and republics. Paciolo traveled from city to city teaching mathematics. Cardano, a medical doctor and mathematician, followed the example of Paciolo and dedicated a chapter of his book on mathematics to the subject of mercantile bookkeeping. These men made no original contribution to bookkeeping; their greatest service was in diffusing the knowledge of double entry the world over.

53

The literature on double entry divides itself into three cycles. The first covers the period from 1458 to 1558. During this century, writers were intent on setting forth the mechanics of bookkeeping as developed by business. No one attempted to develop a theory of double entry and no one went beyond the bookkeeping needs of the mercantile firm. In the second cycle, extending from 1559 to 1795, a new element appeared — the critique of bookkeeping. This was also the period when double entry extended its field of application to other types of organizations, such as monasteries and the state. With the critique and the widening sphere of bookkeeping, began theoretical research into the subject. The third cycle extends from 1796 to the present time. It has seen the development of a complete theory of accounts; bookkeeping has evolved into the practice of accounting.[1]

BENEDETTO COTRUGLIO RAUGEO

The first to write on double entry was probably Benedetto Cotrugli, a native of Dalmatia. He was urged to write his book, *Della mercatura et del mercante perfetto*, by a certain Francesco Stefani, a merchant of Ragusa, to whom his work was dedicated. In its dedication he says that he was often interrupted in the writing because of his many duties and was for a time uncertain in which language to write: whether it was to be in Latin, because more noble and dignified, or in vulgar Italian, because more intelligible to merchants. He decided on the latter.

Cotrugli finished his book on the 25th of August, 1458, and it lay unpublished at Ragusa for more than a century, until a certain Giovanni Giuseppe had a copy made and brought it to Venice, where it was published in 1573.

The book is a small treatise on the institutions of commerce. It is well conceived. Bookkeeping is only touched upon briefly in a short chapter, but enough is said to establish the identity of double entry.

Cotrugli recognizes the importance of having a reliable set of books and advises all merchants unfamiliar with bookkeeping to learn the art or to hire a bookkeeper. A merchant should never depend solely on memory, lest his business soon degenerate into chaos.[2]

Cotrugli says that a merchant should have three books: A *quaderno* (ledger), a *giornale* (journal), and a *memoriale* (memorandum book).

The *quaderno* should have an index so that all entries can be traced readily. God's name should be invoked on the first page. The merchant's name and the number of pages composing the ledger should also appear on the first page. The same alphabetical letter should be clearly marked on the *quaderno*, *alfabetto* (index), *giornale*, and *memoriale*.[3]

Cotrugli says nothing about an inventory,[4] but he does state that the capital

54

is entered in detail in the *giornale* and that from there it is posted to the *quaderno*.[5] He advises the merchant to keep a *libriccino piccolo delle recordanze* (small memorandum book), in which to jot down all transactions as they arise, preparatory to entering them each day in the *memoriale* and *giornale*, and strongly recommends a daily posting to the *quaderno*.[6] At the end of every year, the entries in the *quaderno* should be carefully checked to the *giornale*, and a *bilancione* (this probably is a trial balance and not a balance-sheet) should be drawn up. All the profits and losses should be carried to the capital account.[7]

When the *quaderno* is completed, all open accounts should be closed and their balances carried to an account opened on the last page for this purpose. This balance account is then transferred to a new *quaderno*.[8]

Cotrugli also says that a merchant should keep two other books in which to enter copies of all letters sent out, one for bills delivered and the other for miscellaneous letters. All letters received should be filed according to the general merchants' custom.[9]

These general statements are all that Cotrugli says of double entry. He observes that to treat the subject in detail would be difficult to accomplish in writing. Besides, he says, it is almost impossible to learn bookkeeping without the aid of oral teaching.[10]

The importance of Cotrugli's book lies not so much in its intrinsic worth as in the time when it was written. It antedates Paciolo's work by 36 years![11]

FRA LUCA PACIOLO

Double entry, in the form current at Venice in the fifteenth century, was set forth for the first time in sufficient detail and exactness in the renowned *Distinctio Nona — Tractatus XI, Particularis de computis et scripturis*, included by Luca Paciolo in his *Summa de arithmetica geometria proportioni et proportionalita*, which was published at Venice in 1494.

Paciolo is not only the first significant writer on double entry, but is also the most important one of this first period. His book carried the knowledge of double entry beyond the boundaries of Italy and caused it to be known as the Venetian method.

Paciolo was born at San Sepolcro, Tuscany. He became a Franciscan monk and dedicated himself to the study of mathematics and theology. He distinguished himself in both fields and taught the subjects in many cities of Italy. Paciolo was never an accountant.[12] He included the treatise on bookkeeping so that his *Summa de arithmetica* might be complete. There is no direct connection between the two parts, except that bookkeeping in its application requires a knowledge of principles of arithmetic.

These *summa* are characteristic of the period: there were no clear lines of demarcation between sciences, and even the professions were confused with one another. The spirit of observation prevailed during this era, and everything of interest was treasured in ponderous *summae*, treatises, and chronicles. Methods of application soon followed this vast amount of data, and gradually new fields of science emerged with definite boundaries and distinctive names.

The fact that Paciolo never was a bookkeeper causes Fabio Besta [13] to doubt that he could have written on the subject with such clearness and with such a wealth of detail without the help of some unknown author. Paciolo does not name anyone who might have assisted him; on the contrary, he definitely states in his first chapter that the mercantile order was in great need of a treatise on bookkeeping, and sets himself the task of supplying it. [14] He chooses the method of Venice, which, he says, of all existing is certainly the best [15] — another confirmation of the extensiveness and diversity of bookkeeping in Italy. Besta believes that Paciolo could not possibly have acquired such deep knowledge of mercantile books, and doubts that he had the means or the time to secure such intimate familiarity with Venetian business houses and customs as the writer of the treatise appears to possess. True, Paciolo as a youth lived for a few years in Venice with Antonio Rompiasi, a prominent merchant, but during this time he was studying mathematics at the school of Domenico Bragadino and also tutoring the sons of Rompiasi. In any event, he left Venice in 1470 and did not return until 1494, when he was busy publishing his *Summa*. In the twenty-four years' interval, he traveled to Rome, Zara, Padua, Florence, and Assisi; was secretary to cardinals and professor of mathematics and theology; but in no way was he ever engaged in activities dealing with merchants or bookkeeping. [16]

The Venetian method of double entry is described in great detail in the *Tractatus XI, Particularis de computis et scripturis*. The methods used in the Barbarigo books are set forth here in a clear systematic fashion. It begins with an explanation of the *inventario*. This is a list (an inventory) of all the assets and liabilities, which the owner should prepare before he starts business. The items should be arranged according to their "mobility" and value, cash being the first one, because such items are more easily lost than others of a fixed nature. The *inventario* should be completed in one day, or it may cause trouble in the future management of the business. [17]

The familiar *memoriale*, *giornale*, and *quaderno* are next explained. The *memoriale* is a memorandum book where all transactions are entered chronologically, with complete details as to their nature. [18] No attention is paid to form in this book. Anyone who executes a transaction must enter it with full explanations and in the particular monetary unit in which it was concluded. Because the *memoriale* is accessible to all employees of a business, it is recommended that it not include the *inventario*.

The entries of the *memoriale* are then placed in the *giornale*, with a summary of the explanations.[19] All foreign monetary units are reduced to Venetian money. The entries must be duly classified into debits and credits, and everything that is entered in the *giornale* must first be entered in the *memoriale*. The exception, the *inventorio*, is entered directly into the *giornale*.

The *quaderno* is the ledger. It usually has an *alfabeto* (index) to facilitate locating accounts. It is explained that cash is entered on the first page of the *quaderno*, because it is first in the *giornale*. A whole page is allowed for it, since the cash account is more active than any other. The *quaderno* should be properly ruled, depending on the type of money used. If lire, soldi, denari, and piccioli are used, then four columns are needed, plus a fifth for ledger-folio indexing.[20]

All current books should be marked with the same sign so as to be readily distinguishable from account books of other years. The first set of books is usually marked with a cross, and all succeeding sets are marked successively by the letters of the alphabet.[21]

Tracing a transaction through the books will clarify much that is odd and puzzling in Venetian double entry. When a transaction takes place, it is entered in the *memoriale*. It is set down as a mere memorandum with complete details. Form is not considered important here.[22] The bookkeeper, at his leisure, takes the entry from the *memoriale* and places it in the *giornale*. A diagonal line is drawn through the memorandum entry to show that it has been carried into the *giornale*. Form now becomes all-important. The entry is drawn up according to fixed rules and customs. An example will help to show this.[23]

1493 addì 8 Novembre in Venezia

1   1° *Per Cassa di contanti: A Cavedal di me tale, ecc., per contanti*
2   *mi trovo in quella al presente, fra oro e monete, argento e rame di diversi conii, comme appare nel foglio dell'Inventario posto in cassa ecc., in tutto' ducati tanti d'oro, e monete ducati tanti, valgono in tutto, al modo nostro veneziano a oro, cioè a grossi 24 per duc. e piccioli 32 per grosso a lira a oro*   *lira, soldi, grossi, piccioli.*

Venice November 8, 1493

1   Debit cash: Credit capital, etc., for different coins, which appear in
2   the inventory, etc., total Venetian gold ducats valued at 24 grossi per ducat and 32 piccioli per grosso in gold lire   lira, soldi, grossi, piccioli.

This is a journal entry debiting cash and crediting capital, followed by an explanation. The outstanding characteristic is its paragraph form: the debit, credit, and explanation are placed together in one continuous paragraph. Nevertheless, the debits and credits are carefully segregated. The debit is preceded by the preposition *Per*, which stands for debit, and the credit by the preposition *A*, which stands for credit; [24] the debit and credit being then separated by a colon (:) or two vertical lines (| |).[25] Then follows the explanation, which is a digest of the transaction as entered in the *memoriale*. The money amount is placed at the end of the entry on the right-hand side of the page. The date is always placed at the top of the entry, though the year is placed at the top of the page. This form of journal entry, which was the result of evolution, as shown in part I, had now been rigidly fixed by custom.

Another peculiarity of the practice of Paciolo's time was that there were no compound journal entries. All were simple entries — one debit and credit. If a transaction was a complicated one involving more than one debit or credit, it was split into as many journal entries as there were debits or credits. This procedure, it will be seen, persisted for a long time.

The cross-reference system used in the illustration is the same as the one encountered in Andrea Barbarigo's journal of 1430. The $\frac{1}{2}$ on the left-hand side of the page refers to the posting of the debit and credit. The top number refers to the debit posting, cash in this case, and the lower number to the credit posting, capital in this case.

With the entry properly written up in the *giornale*, the bookkeeper proceeded to post it in the *quaderno*. All debits were placed on the left side of a double page and the credits on the right. An account, therefore, takes in both sides of a double page. Two examples, a debit and a credit, will facilitate an understanding of the ledger entry: [26]

Jesus MCCCCLXXXXIII

Cassa de' contanti deve dare a dì 8 Novembre per Cavedal, per contanti di più sorti fra oro a monete mi trovo avere in quella in questo presente dì, in tutto. Carta 2ª   L.S.G.P.

Jesus 1493

Debit cash on November 8 and credit capital, for cash in different coins. Credit on page 2.   lire, soldi, grossi, piccioli.

Jesus MCCCCLXXXXIII

Cavedal di me tale, ecc, deve avere a dì 8 novembre per Cassa, per contanti mi trovo in quella fin al dì presente in oro e monete di più sorti in tutto. Carta 1ª.   L.S.G.P.

Jesus 1493

Credit capital on November 8 and debit cash, for cash in different coins. Debit on page 1.   lire, soldi, grossi, piccioli.

The debit is to the cash account, and the credit to the capital account. Form here again is of the first importance. The entries are in paragraph form, and the title appears at the beginning. Then follows *deve dare*, meaning debit, or *deve avere*, meaning credit. Next is the date, with the year at the top of the account. The account title of the other half of the transaction also is given, and is followed by a brief explanation. The entry is then closed with the cross-reference number of the corresponding debit or credit of the transaction and with the money amount placed on the right-hand side of the page. When the postings are made, the bookkeeper draws two diagonal lines through the journal entry, one through the left side of the entry to indicate that the debit has been posted, and the other through the right side to indicate that the credit has been posted.

The cross-reference system used in the ledger has one peculiarity. Instead of the entries' bearing the page number of the journal, they bear the page number of the corresponding debit or credit posting in the ledger. The *quaderno* has cross-references between its debits and credits, but not with the *giornale*. To trace entries from the ledger to the journal, one must use the date as a guide.[27]

The profit calculation is typical of venture accounting, as already explained in part I. The profit is calculated on each venture and the net result is transferred to the profit-and-loss account, which in turn is balanced and carried to the capital account. It is recommended not to journalize closing entries, because they originate in the ledger and, therefore, need not be sent through the journal for posting.[28]

The ledger was usually balanced when it was complete, but rarely at any fixed intervals. In any case, the balancing of the ledger always meant that the open balances were to be transferred to a new ledger, even if the old one was not complete. This ledger balancing, called *saldare il quaderno*, was a tedious operation. Before one could start closing out the ledger, he would have to make sure that it was correct. First it was necessary to check very carefully all journal entries against the ledger. That was best done between two persons. All entries traced to the ledger were checked. If there remained no unchecked entries, it meant that the ledger was correct[29] and the bookkeeper would proceed with the closing. When all accounts had been closed, their balances were transferred to the new *quaderno*, without first sending them through the *giornale* for posting. The two *quaderni* were directly cross-referenced between each other for closing and opening balances.[30] With the old *quaderno* closed, the bookkeeper would then add up all its debits and credits and would get a *summa summarium* (grand total) of both. If the debits equalled the credits, it meant that the *quaderno* was properly closed and correct.[31] This balancing and closing of the *quaderno* had to be done in one day, and no new entries were to be made in the books in the meantime.[32]

It is evident that Paciolo, or whoever wrote the *Tractatus XI, Particularis de computis et scripturis*, did not grasp the full meaning of the trial balance, or he would have drawn it up first, instead of checking the whole journal against the ledger to prove its correctness. Nothing is said about a balance-sheet or division of profits in a *compagnia*. The treatise was obviously written for the single proprietorship; if so, such topics would not have had to be discussed.

DOMENICO MANZONI

The first important work after Paciolo's is Manzoni's *Quaderno doppio col suo giornale, secondo il costume di venezia*, published at Venice in several editions, the first dating from 1534. Manzoni is probably the first author who was also a bookkeeper by profession. He, himself, says that he kept several important sets of books in Venice. [33] Moreover, Manzoni was also a teacher of penmanship, abacus, and bookkeeping. These three subjects, as Alfieri [34] asserts, were invariably taught together by the same teacher.

Manzoni made liberal use of Paciolo's *Tractatus*. Many chapters were copied word for word. The merit of his work lies in what he omitted from Paciolo and in the complete and very instructive set of double-entry books which he added to the text of his book. In this Manzoni revealed his knowledge as a practical accountant.

The principal books of account are the *giornale* and the *quaderno*, [35] the *memoriale* being used by merchants as a secondary book, [36] a change in procedure since Paciolo's time. From its place of equality with the *giornale* and *quaderno*, it had dropped to a subordinate position.

Another change is the introduction of numerous *libretti* (small memorandum books); their use eliminated the need for many separate but similar entries in the *giornale* and *quaderno*. Such entries were conveniently brought together in the several libretti, and at varying intervals were summarized, entered in total in the *giornale*, and posted to the *quaderno*. These *libretti* were subdivisions of the *memoriale* rather than of the *giornale*, and were an effective labor-saving device. Following are a few of the *libretti* used: [37]

1. *Spese minute di casa*
2. *Spese di villa*   4. *Spese di fabriche*
3. *Spese di salariadi*   5. *Intrade di fitti*

1. Household expenses
2. Farm expenses   4. Building expenses
3. Salary expenses   5. Rent income

A journal entry of a summarized *libretto* is set forth below: [38]

1540 adì 31 mazo

129   20   *P*   *Spese de Villa // A Cassa, per più spese fatte in la mia possession*
      1   *da Campo San Piero, per far piantar, fossalar, et altre cose*
          necessarie in quella, da dì p° marzo prossimo passato, fin questo zorno,
          come appar in libro de spese de villa, in tutto d. 65 g. 10.

                                          l. 6 s. 10 g. 10 p.

March 31, 1540

129   20   Debit farm expenses || Credit cash for expenses incurred on my
      1   farm at Campo San Piero, for planting, irrigating, and other
          necessary items, from March 1st to this day, as it appears in the
          memorandum farm-expense book, totaling ducati 65, grossi 10.

                                       l. 6, s. 10, g. 10, p.

This is a debit to farm expenses and a credit to cash for all expenses incurred for the spring sowing. There are several other things to be noted in this journal entry. The debit and credit are separated by a double line (||), and the *Per* is abbreviated to the single letter *P*. Another difference is the cross-reference number. To the time-honored fraction, Manzoni added a consecutive number to all journal entries to facilitate tracing ledger entries into the journal. The new method is to be seen in the ledger postings of the journal entry [39] (p. 20):

Debit entry

129   *Spese de villa, die dar adì 31 Marzo, a Cassa, p. più spese fatte in la mia*
        possession da campo san Piero, per far piantar, fossalar et altre necessarie
        in quella, da adì po Marzo, per fin questo zorno, come appar in libro di
        spese di villa, d. 65 g. 10 p.   *C1 l. 6 s. 10 g. 10 p.*

129   Debit farm expenses on March 31 and credit cash for expenses incurred
        on my farm at Campo San Piero, for planting, irrigating, and other
        necessary items, from March 1st to this day, as it appears in the memo-
        randum farm-expense book, totaling ducati 65, grossi 10.

                            page 1 l. 6, s. 10, g. 10, p.

Credit entry

129   *Ditto, p. Spese de villa d. 65 g. 10*   *C20 l. 6 s. 10 g. 10 p.*

129   Ditto, for farm expenses, ducati 65, g. 10.

                          page 20 l. 6, s. 10, g. 10, p.

61

Ditto stands for *Cassa, a l'incontro die haver adì 31 Marzo* . . . which means "Credit cash on March 31st." Whenever a word or a phrase had to be repeated, it was the general practice of the time to replace it by the word *ditto*.

The number 129 is placed in the ledger at the beginning of the entries; the *C1* and *C20* at the end of the entries refer to the page numbers of the debit and credit postings in the ledger itself. The *giornale* and the *quaderno* were now completely cross-referenced. [40]

Manzoni, however, did not himself introduce this consecutive numbering of the journal entries into double entry. He got it from the practice of the day. The records of Zuan Antonio Barbarigo (1537) prove this. An example will be quoted from the *giornale:* [41]

MCCCCXXXVII

71 $\frac{6}{11}$ *Per Cassa // A pro' de imprestiti per conto del monte novissimo, contadi da Messer Vido Memo cassier per la paga de settembre presente per il cavedal de duc. 495, g 17 a 2 1/2 per cento, duc. 12 g. 7 p. 12 val*   *lb. j s. iiij, d. viiij p. 12.*

1537

71 $\frac{6}{11}$ Debit cash || Credit interest on public loans of the Monte Novissimo, paid by Messer Vido Memo, cashier, for the September interest payments on our capital investment of ducati 495, grossi 17, which at 2 1/2% amounts to ducati 12, grossi 7, piccioli 12, equaling
           lb. 1, s. 4, d. 9, p. 12.

This is a debit to cash and a credit to profit on investments for interest received on Venetian government loans.

Manzoni again differs from Paciolo in that he journalizes all transfers of nominal accounts to profit and loss. The only transfers he does not journalize are the accounts forwarded from one page to another. Manzoni is probably the first author to make any attempt at a classification of accounts. He divides all accounts into *vive* (alive) and *morte* (dead). By *vive* he means accounts opened to persons, and by *morte* he means all other accounts. [42]

Venture accounting is explained as by Paciolo, except only that here it is amply illustrated by Manzoni's set of double-entry books. Below is an example from the *quaderno* of cloth bought and sold and of the profit realized in the whole deal: [43]

MDXXXX

26 *Zenzeri beledi tenti, die dar adì 15 Marzo, a Cassa contadi, a S. Polo Corner, p. l'amontar de l.1,200, a d. 18 il %, d. 216.*
C1 l. 21 s. 12 g. p.

51 *Adì 2 Aprile, a Pro et danno, p. utile seguido de quelli d. 24 g. p.* *C13 l. 2 s. 8 g. p.*

MDXXXX

50 *Zenzeri beledi tenti, a l'incontro die haver adì 2 Aprile, p. Cassa contadi da S. Ambroso Dal Diamante, p. l.1,200 a d. 20 il %, monta d. 240 g. p.*
C1 l. 24 s. g. p.

1540

26 Debit unbleached common ginger on March 15 and credit cash, for payment made to S. Polo Corner for 1200 lbs. of ginger, at 18 ducati per 100, which amounts to 216 ducati.
p. 1 l. 21, s. 12, g. , p.

51 April 2. Credit profit and loss for profit made on ginger, which amounts to ducati 24, g. p.
p. 13, l. 2, s. 8, g. , p.

1540

50 Credit unbleached common ginger on April 2 and debit cash, per payment received from S. Ambroso Dal Diamente for 1200 lbs. of ginger, sold at 20 ducati per 100, which amounts to 240 ducati. g. p.
p. 1 l. 24, s. , g. , p.

As soon as the original lot of unbleached common ginger (bought on March 15th) was sold on April 2nd, the account was balanced and the profit (*utile*) was transferred into profit and loss (*pro et danno*). The profit-and-loss account was itself closed into the capital account at irregular intervals, ranging anywhere from a few months to several years. These are the principal characteristics of venture accounting.

Manzoni's procedure for the closing of the books is very much the same as Paciolo's. One peculiarity, however, is the way in which he takes off his *summa summarium* (trial balance). Instead of taking only the ultimate total debits and credits of each ledger, he also includes the totals of all accounts that have been balanced and forwarded. Thus, if an account is forwarded two or more times, all the individual totals of the closed accounts are included in the trial balance. An abstract of Manzoni's *summa summarium* is given below: [44]

Summe de tutte le partide poste in quaderno, si in dar, come anche in haver.
(Sum of debit and credit ledger entries.)

Ledger Folio	Debit (*In Dar*)	Credit (*In Haver*)
1. *Cassa de Contadi* Cash	l. 578 s. 16 g. 4 p. 22	l. 578 s. 16 g. 4 p. 22
2. *Cavedal de mi Aloise* *Vallaresso* Capital, A. Vallaresso	l. 2360 s. 16 g. 11 p.	l. 2360 s. 16 g. 11 p.
3. *Bancho di Priulli* Bank of Priulli	l. 263 s. 2 g. 11 p. 22	l. 263 s. 2 g. 11 p. 22
3. *Zoie di più sorte* Various jewels	l. 121 s. 10 g. p.	l. 121 s. 10 g. p.
13. *Pro et Danno* Profit and loss	l. 137 s. 7 g. p.	l. 137 s. 7 g. p.
17. *Spese di viver di casa* Household expenses	l. 4 s. 7 g. 6 p. 13	l. 4 s. 7 g. 6 p. 13
19. *Spese diverse* Miscellaneous expenses	l. 5 s. 18 g. p.	l. 5 s. 18 g. p.
22. *Cassa de contadi* Cash	l. 669 s. 8 g. 11 p. 10	l. 669 s. 8 g. 11 p. 10
25. *Pro et Danno* Profit and loss	l. 120 s. 12 g. 2 p. 21	l. 120 s. 12 g. 2 p. 21
30. *Cassa de contadi* Cash etc.	etc.	etc.
Summa delle Summe l.	s. g. p.	l. s. g. p.

It is clear that the cash account (*cassa de contadi*) and the profit-and-loss account (*pro et danno*) appear more than once in the trial balance, because they have been forwarded several times in the ledger.

Manzoni, as well as Paciolo, fell into a grave error when he took off his *summa summarium:* both drew up the trial balance of the old ledger only after it had been completely balanced, closed, and all open accounts transferred to the new ledger. It was thus bound to balance in all cases, even if the ledger were full of errors, because both sides of the accounts were made equal by transferring their balance to the new ledger. A trial balance of these closed ledger accounts was not a true trial balance at all; it proved nothing. This is clearly seen in the example. Neither the true function of the trial balance nor its proper construction were known in the early sixteenth century.

In all single ownerships of this period, domestic accounts were included in the ledger, along with the other business accounts, and were closed into profit and loss just as all other nominal accounts were. It was natural for owners of a small business to include their personal household expenses in their business accounts, for they did not distinguish between their business and their domestic activities. The business did not have an entity of its own, but was inextricably interwoven with the domestic life of its owner. Even gambling results were regularly included in the profit-and-loss account.

An interesting example of this intermingling of accounts is Manzoni's handling of dowry and marriage expenses on his books: [45]

1540 Adì 15 Ottubrio

208 $\frac{33}{34}$ *P Cavedal de mi Aloise Vallaresso // A. S. Jacomo Bragadin mio cugnado, per tanti gli ho promesso, per conto de la dota de Faustina mia sorella, tra robba et dinari, come per il contratto de la nozze appar d. 4000 g. p.*   *val. l. 400 s. g. p.*

October 15, 1540

208 $\frac{33}{34}$ Debit Capital || Credit S. Jacomo Bragadino, my brother-in-law, for the dowry I promised him for my sister Faustina, as shown in marriage contract, amounting to 4,000 ducati g. p. which equals
l. 400 s. , g. , p.

He promised to pay his sister's dowry, so he charged his capital account and credited his brother-in-law for the amount. But when he, himself, got married, he debited his father-in-law and credited capital for the dowry due him, as is shown in the entry below: [46]

1540 adì 30 Ottubrio

216 $\frac{35}{36}$ *P. S. Philippo Moresini, mio succero // A Rason di dota, de Lucretia mia moier, d. 4000 che lui mi promesse per conto di dota, computado d. 400 de Zoie, et d. 350 de vestimenti per suo uso, come appar nel contratto de le noze fatto per S. Marcho Baldi, golo de nozze.*   *Val. l. 400 s. g. p.*

October 30, 1540

216 $\frac{35}{36}$ Debit S. Philippo Moresini, my father-in-law || Credit dowry of Lucretia, my wife, for 4,000 ducati promised to me by my father-in-law, included among which are jewels worth 400 ducati and 350 ducati for her personal trousseau, as shown in the marriage contract drawn up by Marcho Baldi.   l. 400 s. , g. , p.

The account, *rason de dota*, is a clearing account, debited for all the marriage expenses and credited with the dowry. The net balance of the account was in the end transferred to the capital account.

GEROLAMO CARDANO

Cardano published his *Practica arithmetica* in 1539, and emulated Paciolo in devoting a chapter, entitled *De ratione librorum*, to double entry. In fact, it is a condensed summary of Paciolo's *Tractatus*. The book is written in Latin. A return to Latinism was characteristic of the fifteenth and sixteenth centuries. Even Cotrugli, as previously mentioned, was in doubt whether to write in Latin or vulgar Italian. Cardano contributed nothing to our knowledge of the bookkeeping of the day. His chapter on double entry is no more than twelve paragraphs, merely a brief outline of the subject.[47]

ALVISE CASANOVA

Casanova was a teacher of bookkeeping, official accountant to the Venetian Republic, and a private accountant. His vast experience stood him in good stead when he wrote his book on double entry: *Specchio lucidissimo nel quale si vedono essere diffinito tutti i modi, e ordini de scrittura, che si deve menare nelli negotiamenti della mercantia*. An important work of this first period of accounting literature, it was published at Venice in 1558.

Casanova, primarily a practical accountant, gives little attention to theory. His book consists mainly of an illustrative set of double-entry books developed by him, with brief explanations here and there clarifying intricate points of procedure. It merits close attention, for it introduces several novel features.[48]

The *memoriale* is here omitted completely from bookkeeping for the first time. In the span of a century, it had fallen from its place of eminence as one of the three principal books to complete oblivion. Cotrugli and Paciolo classed it as essential; Manzoni, though still using it, minimized its importance; Casanova simply ignored its existence. The necessary account books, says Casanova, are the *giornale* and the *libro* (ledger — another name for *quaderno*).[49]

On the whole, the *giornale* does not differ from its predecessors. Casanova ignores Manzoni's consecutively numbered journal entries and reverts to Paciolo's method of cross-indexing journal and ledger entries, as is seen in the following example:[50]

MDLV *adì 5 Marzo*

$\frac{3}{4}$ *Per Nave sopraditta (l. e. Zanfort) // a S. Batista Balarin per conto et come perzenevole di quella d. 2500, il facciamo creditor, per caratti 6, il participa in essa nave, i qual sono stati per lui sborsati come appar per il ditto nostro instrumento*   *val l. 250 s.   g.   p.*

March 5, 1555

3
—
4

Debit ship Zanfort || Credit S. Batista Balarin for his share in the ship, which is 6/24 of the total venture, and for which he paid 2,500 ducati in cash, as shown in the contract.   l. 250 s.   , g.   , p.   [51]

This is a debit to the ship Zanfort, and a credit to S. Batista Balarin for his share of 6/24 in the venture undertaken.

The *giornale* differs from earlier forms in one important respect: it is subdivided into special journals or memorandum journals, called *giornaletti* or *libri*. Since Casanova omitted the *memoriale*, he also had to omit the *libretti*, which were special *memoriale* books. The *giornaletti* are of a similar nature, but have the distinguishing characteristic of being subdivisions of the journal. They are not full-fledged journals, however, because when summarized they have to be entered in the *giornale* before being posted to the ledger. A summary of a *giornaletto*, as taken from the journal, is quoted below: [52]

MDLV adì 31 Mazo

14
—
1

Per Spese per uso del viver de casa // a Cassa d. 15 g. 20 p. 10 contadi, per più spese fatte nelli infrascritti mesi tre, si come appar nel giornaletto delle spese a questo deputato, et sottoscritto, a mese per mese, esser state portade nel libro in questo giorno, et prima.

Per il mese de marzo per la summa de	L. 34 S. 16
Per il mese de Aprille	L. 31 s. 14
Per il mese de Mazo	L. 32 s. 15
Suma in tutto (lire piccioli o comune)	L. 98 s. 5
Fanno a correnti li sopraditti	val. l. 1 s. 11 g. 8 p. 10

May 31, 1555

14
—
1

Debit household expenses || Credit cash for d. 15, g. 20, p. 10, for miscellaneous expenses incurred in the past three months, as shown in the household expense *giornaletto*, and as is shown in detail below:

For the month of March	L. 34 s. 16
For the month of April	L. 31 s. 14
For the month of May	L. 32 s. 15
Grand total (in common lire)	L. 98 s. 5
This sum is equivalent to	l. 1 s. 11 g. 8 p. 10

Domestic expenses are debited and cash credited. The source of this journal entry was the *giornaletto* of household expenditures.

55   **MDLV**

Resti di questo Libro denno dar adi
28 Febraro per Mobile et Arnese

di Casa	C. 3	L. 99	s. 5	g. 10	p.	
ditto, per Banco de S. Daniel et Andrea Dolfin	C. 40	L. 763	s. 1	g. 6	p. 30	
ditto, per S. Bortolamio de Righin	C. 46	L. 65	s. 12	g.	p.	
ditto, per S. Lorenzo di Scudi	C. 46	L. 70	s. 12	g.	p.	
ditto, per S. Adolfo Settlin	C. 48	L.	s. 1	g. 1	p.	
ditto, per S. Bortolamio	C. 49	L. 1	s.	g. 2	p. 20	
ditto, per Cassa de contadi	C. 51	L. 2318	s. 6	g. 4	p. 2	
ditto, per Lane Gotis gualde et Moiane	C. 44	L. 235	s. 2	g. 8	p.	
ditto, per Seda Valona	C. 53	L. 80	s. 4	g.	p.	
ditto, per Seda della Morea	C. 54	L. 186	s. 8	g.	p.	
ditto, per Diamanti Grezi	C. 54	L. 83	s. 6	g.	p.	

Summa L. 3902 s. 19 g. 8 p. 20

MDLV

Resti di questo Libro di a haver adi 28
Febraro per Cavedal de noi

Vielmo et Zuane Zanfort	C. 2	L. 2998	s. 10	g. 10	p. 3	
ditto, per pro et Danno	C. 53	L. 904	s. 8	g. 10	p. 17	

Summa L. 3902 s. 19 g. 8
p. 20

1555

Debit balance of this ledger and credit
on Feb. 28:

ditto, Furniture and fixtures	P. 3	L. 99	s. 5	g. 10	p.	
ditto, Bank of S. Daniel & Andrea Dolfin	P. 40	L. 763	s. 1	g. 6	p. 30	
ditto, S. Bortolamio de Righin	P. 46	L. 65	s. 12	g.	p.	
ditto, S. Lorenzo di Scudi	P. 40	L. 70	s. 12	g.	p.	
ditto, S. Adolfo Settlin	P. 40	L.	s. 1	g. 1	p.	
ditto, S. Bortolamio	P. 49	L. 1	s.	g. 2	p. 20	
ditto, Cash	P. 51	L. 2318	s. 6	g. 4	p. 2	
ditto, Wool	P. 44	L. 235	s. 2	g. 8	p.	
ditto, Branch at Valona	P. 53	L. 80	s. 4	g.	p.	
ditto, Branch at Morea	P. 54	L. 186	s. 8	g.	p.	
ditto, Rough Diamonds	P. 54	L. 83	s. 6	g.	p.	

Total L. 3902 s. 19 g. 8 p. 20

1555

Credit balances of this ledger and
debit on Feb. 28

ditto, Capital of Vilemo a Zuane	p. 2	L. 2998	s. 10	g. 10	p. 3	
ditto, Profit & loss	p. 53	L. 904	s. 8	g. 10	p. 17	

Total L. 3902 s. 19 g. 8 p. 20

Casanova introduced the practice of journalizing closing entries and transfers of open accounts between ledgers. He eliminated the direct ledger closing of nominal accounts, as Manzoni did, but went one step further in eliminating direct transfers between ledgers, without routing them first through the journal.

Casanova's greatest innovation was his totally new technique of closing the ledger (*saldare il libro*). He started by closing all completed ventures and other nominal accounts into the profit-and-loss account. Venture accounts were closed only at the end of the fiscal year, a sharp departure from the previous practice of closing such accounts at the termination of each venture. The next step called for the opening of a balance account, called *resti di questo libro*. In here, were transferred all open accounts of the ledger. When this was done, the ledger was completely closed and balanced. On page sixty-eight is an example of a balance account,[53] containing all the open ledger accounts. The profit-and-loss account was not transferred to capital, but was closed directly into *resti di questo libro*. It is clear that the balance account closed the ledger.

Casanova did not use the clumsy *summa summarium* of Paciolo and Manzoni and therefore avoided its errors. He does not have any substitute for it, but the balance account was a true post-closing trial balance. Casanova apparently did not know this, for he never mentioned it as a proof of the correctness of the ledger, but merely as a convenient medium for closing the ledger. Nevertheless, his ledger-closing procedure was correct and a distinct advance over the method used by his predecessors.

To open the new ledger, his procedure was reversed. The balance account was entered in the new journal and posted to the ledger, but in the reverse order. What were debits in the old balance account became credits in the new one, and vice versa. This is evident for he used the account to open the ledger. The example on page seventy shows this.[54] This is like the balance account of the old ledger reversed. All the entries in the account are journalized, and their corresponding debits and credits are formally opened in the ledger. The balance account naturally balances and is therefore closed. The ledger is now ready for the business of the new fiscal period.

GIOVANNI ANTONIO TAGLIENTE

Tagliente was a man of varied activities. He never was a mathematician of Paciolo's calibre, nor was he ever a merchant, but made his living by teaching and writing on anything that held a lure of profit. He helped his father write a book of arithmetic, *Libro d'abaco che insegna a fare ogni raxon mercadantile*. His other writings include a strange assortment of topics, ranging from the art of penmanship to love letters, embroidery, and a new method on how to learn to read in a short time.[55]

1.

Resti tratti dal Libro A, denno dar adi primo Marzo, per Cavedal de noi Vielmo et Zuane Zanfort fratelli della Citta d'Anversa d. 29985 g. 10 p. 3 facciamo debitori ditti resti per altretanti che in ditto Libro gli habbiamo fatti creditori. C. 2 L. 2998 s. 10 g. 10 p. 3
ditto, per Pro et Danno C. 2 L. 904 s. 8 g. 10 p. 17
Summa L. 3902 s. 19 g. 8 p. 20

1555

Debit on March 1st Balances of ledger A and credit capital of Vielmo and Zuane Zanfort, brothers from the city of Antwerp for d. 29,985 g. 10, p. 3 and the balance of this account, which were credited in ledger here P. 2 L. 2998 s. 10 g. 10 p. 3
Profit and loss P. 2 L. 904 s. 8 g. 10 p. 17
Total L. 3902 s. 19 g. 8 p. 20

JESU CHRISTI MDLV

Resti tratti del Libro A, denno haver adi primo Marzo per Mobile et Arnese di Casa d. 992 g. 22 facciamo creditori ditti resti per altritanti che in ditto Libro gli habbiamo fatti debitori C. 2 L. 99 s. 5 g. 10 p. 30
ditto, per Banco de S. Daniel et Andre Dolfin C. 2 L. 763 s. 1 g. 6 p.
ditto, per S. Bortolomio de Righin C. 2 L. 65 s. 12 g. p.
ditto, per S. Lorenzo di Scudi C. 2 L. 70 s. 12 g. p.
ditto, per S. Adolfo Settlin C. 3 L. s. 1 g. 1 p.
ditto, per S. Bortolamio Andronico C. 3 L. 1 s. g. 2 p. 20
ditto, per Cassa de contadi C. 3 L. 2318 s. 6 g. 4 p. 2
ditto, per Lane Gotis gualde et Moiane C. 3 L. 235 s. 2 g. 8 p.
ditto, per Seda Valona C. 3 L. 80 s. 4 g. p.
ditto, per Seda della Morea C. 3 L. 186 s. 8 g. p.
ditto, per Diamanti Grezi C. 3 L. 83 s. 6 g. p.
Summa L. 3902 s. 19 g. 8 p. 20

1555

Credit on March 1st balances of ledger A and debit furniture and fixtures for d. 992 g. 22, the balances of this account which were debited in ledger A are credited here P. 2 L. 99 s. 5 g. 10 p. 30
ditto, Bank of S. Daniel & Andrea Dolfin P. 2 L. 763 s. 1 g. 6 p. 30
ditto, S. Bortolamio de Righin P. 2 L. 65 s. 12 g. p.
ditto, S. Lorenzo di Scudi P. 2 L. 70 s. 12 g. p.
ditto, S. Adolfo Settlin P. 3 L. s. 1 g. 1 p.
ditto, S. Bortolamio Andronico P. 3 L. 1 s. g. 2 p. 20
ditto, Cash P. 3 L. 2318 s. 6 g. 4 p. 2
ditto, Woll P. 3 L. 235 s. 2 g. 8 p.
ditto, Branch at Valona P. 3 L. 80 s. 4 g. p.
ditto, Branch at Morea P. 3 L. 186 s. 8 g. p.
ditto, Rough diamonds P. 3 L. 83 s. 6 g. p.
Total L. 3902 s. 19 g. 8 p. 20

Amid this variety of subjects, Tagliente published in 1525 his *Luminario di arithmetica, libro doppio.* It is a slender pamphlet on double entry, containing nothing new and much inferior to the work published by Paciolo. Tagliente gives only an example of a *giornale*, briefly prefaced by an explanation of how to set up a *quaderno*,[56] in which he mentions the *Per* and *A*, the segregating of debits and credits in the ledger, the correct placement of the date and cross-reference numbers. He does not, however, give any illustration of the *quaderno* and does not explain how a ledger should be opened, closed, or profits determined. With the exception of this brief introductory paragraph, Tagliente writes no word on how to keep a set of books. He does not even allude to a *memoriale* or any other type of memorandum book. He gives a short example of an *inventario*, which he calls *aventario*, but makes no distinction between assets and liabilities, and gives no attention to the net capital of the business.

Aventario

Danaria contadi	ducati.	500
In bancho di capelli evendramini	"	400
In mobele de casa	"	200
In stabele	"	10,000
In possession campi cento stimadi duc. 12 el campo	"	1,200
In la camera dimprestiti duc. 5,000 stimadi a 40 el cento	"	2,000
Pro dimpresti duc. 200 stimadi duc. 60 el cento	"	120
Canele longi lire 800 stimadi duc. 20 el cento	"	160
Per debitor sier bernardo bolani duc. 500	"	500
Per creditor sier Vizenzo Zorzi duc. 250	"	250

Inventory

Cash	ducati	500
Bank of Capelli Evendramini	"	400
Furniture and fixtures	"	200
Real estate	"	10,000
Land — 100 lots at 12 duc. each	"	1,200
Public loan, 5,000 duc. par, market value 40 duc. per 100	"	120
Cane cinnamon, 800 par, valued at 20 per 100	"	160
Account receivable, Bernardo Bolani, duc. 500	"	500
Account payable, Vinzenzo Zorzi, duc. 250	"	250

The journal entries are also not up to the standard set by Paciolo. An example is quoted below:[57]

Per panni bressani, A, Sier Francesco Zane p. peze 56 e dui terzi a d. 30 la peza monti ducati 1,700 a baratto de stagni a ducati 68 el miaro.

ual l 170   g.   p.

Debit Brescian cloth, credit ser Francesco Zane for 56 2/3 bolts at 30 denari per bolt (equals 1700 ducati) in exchange for zinc valued at 68 per thousand. Valued at 170 lire, d.   , g.   , p.

This is a receipt of cloth in exchange for zinc delivered to Francesco Zane. Tagliente seems to forget the sketchy rules he inserted at the beginning of the *Giornale*, because he has no date in his journal entries and he does not make use of a cross-index system. He also differs from Paciolo in that he does not use any device, such as a colon or lines, to separate the debit and credit of journal entries.

ANONYMOUS WRITERS

There are two pamphlets by anonymous authors, one published in 1525 and the other in 1529. Each is of little importance. Neither goes beyond ten pages and nothing more is given than a faulty, meager outline of the mechanics of double entry. Theory is untouched. Both authors, however, try to make up their deficiencies with long pompous titles. The first being: "*Opera che insegna a tener conti de libro secondo lo consueto di tutti li lochi della Italia, al modo mercantile. La qual opera, prima v'insegna a notare le partite delle comprede et vendite. Et de sapper notar le partite del schotere et del pagare. Et ancora a sapper notare le partite delle pigione delle case et possessioni. Et ancora a sapper tener conto de spese de casa ordinariamente per poter in capo dell'anno render buon conto a cui fusti obbligato. Et più a saper notare molte altre partite, come nell'opera vederete.*" ("Method on how to keep books according to the customs of the various parts of Italy. It includes purchases and sales, accounts receivable and payable, rents, and possessions, and household expenditures. It shows many other things, as you will see in the book.")

And the second: "*Opera che insegna a tener libro doppio et a far partite, e ragion de Banchi, e de Mercante, a riportar le partite, etc. . . .*" [58] ("Method on how to keep a ledger, make entries, bank and mercantile transactions, transferring of accounts, etc. . . .")

BARTOLOMEO FONTANA

The next work on double entry is Fontana's *Ammaestramento novo che insegna a tener libro ordinariamente ad uso di questa città di venetia, comme etiam di tutta l'italia*. It appeared in Venice in 1551. The pamphlet, only eight pages, is an exceedingly bad summary of Tagliente's rather inferior work. As might be expected, it contains nothing new on double entry. [59]

CONCLUSION

Out of the review of accounting literature for the century ending in 1558, the fact emerges that bookkeeping practices then current in business were far superior to treatises on the subject. The writers contributed nothing original. They did not attempt to develop a rationale of double entry, but merely observed that, in practice, bookkeeping followed a more or less well defined procedure.

In the second period, accounting literature takes a new turn. The rise of an accounting critique and the extension of double entry usages to new types of enterprise gradually gave accounting literature the stamp of originality.

NOTES

[1] Bariola. Op. cit., part 2, chap. 13.

[2] Cotrugli, Benedetto Raugeo, *Della mercatura et del mercante perfetto.* (Venice, 1573) Chap. 13, p. 73. "*Et però admonisco, e conforto ogni mercante che si diletti di saper bene, e con ordine tenir li suoi libri, e chi non sa facciasi insegnare, o veramente tengi un sufficiente, e pratico giovane quaderniero. Altrimenti le tue mercantie saranno un caos, e una confusione Babbilonica . . . il mercante non si debba confidare nella memoria, la quale fiducia fece molti errare.*"

[3] Ibid. Chap. 13, p. 70. "*Debbe adunque il mercante tenere tre libri, cioè il quaderno, giornale e memoriale. Il quale quaderno debbe havere 'l' suo Alfabetto: per il quale si possa trovare presto ogni partita scritta nel detto Quaderno: Et essere segnato con A, e in su la prima carta d'esso invocare il nome di Dio, e di chi è, di quante carte ch'egl'è, segnando etiando col'detto A, il suo giornale, Alfabetto e memoriale.*"

[4] See Paciolo on the meaning of inventory.

[5] Ibid. Chap. 13, p. 71. "*Nel giornale formerai per ordine cosa per cosa, tutto 'l capitale, et lo riporterai nel, quaderno.*"

[6] Ibid. Chap. 13, p. 72. "*Avvertendo ancora, che tu abbia a tenire sempre appresso di te un libriccino piccolo delle ricordanze; nel qual noterai giornalmente, et hora per infino li minuti de tuoi negotij, per poter con tua maggior comodità, poi creare le partite in sul libro del memoriale, ovvero giornale, sforzandoti di sempre riportarle dal detto Memoriale tutte, o parte d'esse quell'istesso giorno, o l'altro in sul giornale; poi giornalmente riportarle in sul quaderno.*"

[7] Ibid. Chap. 13, p. 72. "*Et a capo d'ogni anno lo scontrarai con le partite d'esso suo giornale, levando, il bilancione d'esse, et riportando tutti gli avanzi overo disavanzi alla partita del tuo cappitale.*"

[8] Ibid. Chap. 13, p. 71. ". . . *et finito c'haverai di scrivere tutto 'l detto quaderno salderai in esso tutte le partite accese, tirando d'esse tutti li resti, si del debito, come anche del credito, all'ultimo foglio appresso della ultima partita. Riportandoli poi in nuovo quaderno, dando a ciascheduno resto la sua partita da per se . . .*"

[9] Ibid. Chap. 13, p. 72. "*Debbi ancora tenir due altri libri, l'uno per accopiar li conti che mandano di fuori, l'altro per accopiar le tue lettere missive: per infino della minima impor- tantia, . . . et a tutte le lettere che ricevi . . . conservandole ivi secondo costumano fare li veri mercanti.*"

[10] Ibid. Chap. 13, p. 73. "*Et questo per brevità, basti haver detto dell'ordine de libri, et scritture, che a voler narrar qui'l tutto minutamente sarei troppo prolisso, e quasi impossibile a esprimerle, che senza la viva voce, per scrittura difficilmente si può imparare.*"

[11] Ibid. Chap. 13, p. 70.
    Bariola. Op. cit., part 2, p. 363.
    Besta. Op. cit., vol. 3, p. 360.
[12] See footnote 15.
[13] Besta. Op. cit., vol. 3, pp. 363–376.
[14] Paciolo, Luca, *Summa de arithmetica* (Venice, 1494), chap. 1. ". . . *rivolgendosi a tutto l'ordine mercantesco: deliberai (oltre le cose dinance in questa nostra opera ditte) ancor particular tractato grandemente necessario compillare, E in questo solo lo inserto: perchè a ogni loro occorrença el presente libro possa servire.*"
[15] Ibid. Chap. 1. "*E servaremo in esso il modo di Vinegia, quale certamente fra gli altri è molto da commendare e mediante quello in ogni altro si possa guidare.*"
[16] Besta. Op. cit., vol. 3, p. 361.
    Bariola. Op. cit., part 2, p. 366.
    There is a considerable controversy about Paciolo's authorship of the *Tractatus XI, Particularis de computis et scripturis*. Weighty arguments are set forth supporting both sides of the question, but the complete absence of all traces of an earlier manuscript which Paciolo could have copied bars the question from being decisively answered. Eduard Weber, on page 7 of his *Literaturgeschichte der handelsbetriebslehre* (Tübingen, 1914), cites P. Rigobon, *Studii antichi e moderni interno alla tecnica dei commerci* (Bari, 1902), as authority for the statement that the *Tractatus* is taken practically in its entirety from a manuscript of one L. di Chiarini.
    Balduin Penndorf in his book, *Luca Pacioli abhandlung über die buchhaltung 1494*, published in 1933, pp. 63–82, supports Besta in several of his arguments, but disagrees with him in many of the others, principally because Besta and Vianello maintain that Paciolo had no mercantile experience. Penndorf says that, if they had paid closer attention to Paciolo's other sections of the *Summa*, they would have seen that in several instances he makes detailed analysis of Venetian mercantile transactions, thus showing that he did possess an intimate knowledge of the commercial practices of the day. Penndorf, however, makes no definite commitment as to Paciolo's authorship of the *Tractatus*, though the fact that the trend of his arguments run counter to Besta's suggests that he is of the opinion that Paciolo did write the *Tractatus*.
[17] Paciolo. Op. cit., chap. 2. "*E però prima conviene che faccia suo diligente Inventario in questo modo, che sempre scriva in un foglio, ovvero libro da parte, ciò che si ritrova avere al mondo di mobile e di stabile, cominciando sempre dalle cose che sono in più pregio e più labili al perdere, come sono i denari contanti, cioè argenti, ecc., perchè gli stabili come sono, case, terreni, lagune, valli, peschiere e simili, non si possono smarrire come le cose mobili. E successivamente poi di mano in mano scrivere l'altre, ponendo sempre prima il dì, il milesimo, il luogo, il nome suo nel detto Inventario; e tutto detto Inventario si deve tenere in un medesimo giorno perchè altramente darebbe travaglio nel maneggio futuro.*"
[18] Ibid. Chap. 6. "*Onde Memoriale, ovvero secondo alcuni Vacchetta, ovvero Squartafoglio è un libro nel quale tutte le faccende sue il mercadante, piccole e grandi che a mano gli vengono a giorno per giorno, a ora per ora, scrive, nel qual diffusamente ogni cosa di vendere e comprare (e altri maneggi) scrivendo si dichiara non lasciando un jota, il chi, il che, il quando, il dove, con tutte chiarezze e menzioni . . .*"
[19] Ibid. Chap. 10. "*Ma le partite del ditto giornale si convengono formare e dittare per altro modo più leggiadro, non superfluo, neanche troppo di minuto . . .*"
[20] Ibid. Chap. 13. ". . . *Quaderno grande, il quale comunemente si costuma fare di due tante carte che il giornale, nel quale converrà essere uno Alfabeto, ovvero Repertorio o trovarello, se vuoi dire secondo alcuni; alla fiorentina si lo Stratto . . . E nella prima sua carta dentro porrai debitrice la cassa, siccome ella è la prima nel giornale, così deve essere prima nel Quaderno. E tutta quella facciata si costuma lasciarla stare per ditta Cassa, e in dare ne in avere non si pone altro; e questo perchè la Cassa si maneggia più che partita che sia a ora per ora, in mettere e cavar denari; e poi li si lascia il campo largo. E questo Quaderno convien che sia rigato di tante righe quante sorte di monete vuoi trar fuori. Se trarrai lire, soldi, denari, piccioli, farrai quattro righe, ed innanzi alle lire ne farai un'altra per mattervi il numero delle carte delle partite che insieme di dare e avere s'incatenano . . .*"

ACCOUNTING LITERATURE: THE FIRST CYCLE (1458–1558)

[21] Ibid. Chap. 6. *"E però bene si costuma fra i veri cattolici segnare i primi loro libri di quel glorioso segno . . . della Santa Croce . . . E poi i seguenti libri segnerai per ordine d'alfabeto, cioè di A e poi i terzi di B, discorrendo per ordine d'alfabeto."*
[22] Ibid. Chap. 8.
[23] Ibid. Chap. 12.
[24] See chap. 3, footnote 4.
[25] Paciolo. Chap. 11. *"Due sono (come è ditto) i termini usitati in ditto Giornale, l'uno ditto 'Per,' e l'altro è ditto 'A'; i quali hanno loro significati ciascuno separato. Per lo 'Per' sempre si dinota il debitore, o uno o più che si sieno; e per 'A' si dinota il creditore, o uno o più che si sieno. E mai si mette partita ordinaria in Giornale (che al Libro grande s'abbia a porre) che non se ne dinoti prima per i ditti due termini. Dei quali sempre nel principio di ciascuna partita si mette il 'Per' poichè prima si deve specificare il debitore, e dippoi immediate il suo creditore diviso l'un dall'altro per due virgolette (//) . . ."*
[26] Ibid. Chap. 15.
[27] Ibid. Chap. 14. *"Per la qual cosa sappi che di tutto le partite che tu avrai poste nel giornale al quaderno grande, te ne convion sempre fare due, cioè una in dare e l'altra in avere perchè li si chiama lo debitore per lo 'Per' e lo creditore per lo 'A' come di sopra dicemmo; che dell'uno e dell'altro si deve da per se fare una partita, quella del debitore ponere alla man sinistra e quella del creditore alla man destra, e in quella del debitore chiamare la carta dove sia quella del suo creditore, e così in quella del creditore chiamare la carte di quella dove sia il debitore; e in questo modo sempre vengono incatenate tutte le partite del ditto quaderno grande, nel quale mai si deve mettere cosa in dare che quella ancora non si ponga in avere, e così mai si deve mettere cosa in avere che ancora quella medesima con suo ammontare non si metta in dare. E di quà nasce poi il bilancio, che del libro si fa nel suo saldo: tanto convien che sia il dare quanto l'avere, cioè sommate tutte le partite che saranno poste in dare, se fossero bien 10,000, da parte, in su un foglio, a dippoi si sommate similmente tutte quelle che in avere si trovano, tanto debbe fare l'una somma quanto l'altra; altramente dimostrerebbe essere errore nel ditto quaderno, come nel modo del far suo bilancio si dirà a pieno."*
[28] Ibid. Chap. 17. *"Seguita dopo ogni altra partita una chiamata di Pro e Danno o vuoi dire Utile e Danno, ovvero Avanzi e Disavanzi secondo alcuno paese, nella quale tutte le altre del tuo Quaderno sempre si hanno a saldare . . . E questo non bisogna si metta in Giornale, ma besta solo nel Quaderno, perchè là nasce in quello delle cose avanzate, ovvero mancate in dare e avere, per la quale dirai: Pro e Danno deve dare e Pro e Danno avere, cioè quando d'alcuna rova avessi perduto, la cui partita più nel tuo Quaderno restasse in dare che in avere, allora aiuterai il suo avere per pareggiarlo al dare, acciò si saldi, di quel tanto che gli mancasse, dicendo e deve avere per Pro e Danno qual qui metto per saldo di questa partita per danno seguito . . . e segnerai le carte del Pro e Danno nel trar fuori la partita. E al Pro e Danno anderai in dare dicendo e Pro e Danno dee dare a dì . . . per la tal roba, per danno seguito tanto . . . posto in quella al dee avere per suo saldo a se a carte. . . E se la fosse più in avere ditta roba che in dare, allora faresti per l'avverso."*
[29] Ibid. Chap. 32. *"Queste cose fin ora ben notate, bisogna ora dar modo al riporto di un Libro in altro, quando volessi mutar Libro per cagion che fosse pieno, ovvero per ordine annuale di millesimo, come il più si costuma fare per luoghi famosi, che ogni anno, massime a millesimi nuovi, i gran mercatanti sempre lo osservano. E questo atto insieme con li seguenti è ditto il Bilancio del Libro. La qual cosa volere seguire, bisogna grandissima diligenza; e per ordine terrai questo modo: cioè prima farai di avere un compagno, che mal potresti per te solo farlo: a lui darai in mano il giornale, per più cautela, e tu terrai il Quaderno grande; e dirai a lui, cominciando dalla 1ª partita del Giornale, che chiami le carte del tuo Quaderno dove quella sia posta, prima in dare e poi in avere, e così tu l'obbidirai e troverai sempre dove ti manda . . . E fatto questo per ordine a tutto il Quaderno e Giornale, e trovando, tu appunto come lui, in dare e avere, le partite saran giuste e ben poste . . . Ma se fornito il Giornale di puntare a te avanzasse in Quaderno partita alcuna che non venisse puntata in dare o in avere, denoteria nel Quaderno essere errore . . ."*
[30] Ibid. Chap. 34. *"Fatto che avrai questo con diligenza, e tu da te salderai tutto il tuo quaderno partita per partita in questo modo, che prima comincierai dalla Cassa, debitori, robe e avventori, e quelle perterai in libro A, cioè in Quaderno nuovo, che non bisogna, come*

75

fu ditto di sopra, i reſti ponere in Giornale. Sommerai tutte lor partite, in dare e in avere, aiutando sempre la minore come ti dissi sopra del portare avanti; che queſto atto di un Quaderno nell'altro è di punto simile a quello, e fra loro non è altra differenza, se non che in quello il reſto si porta avanti nel medesimo Quaderno, e in queſto da un libro nell'altro, e dove in quello chiamavi le carte di quel Libro proprio, in queſto si chiama la carte del libro seguente, in modo che nel ripporto di un libro nell'altro solo una volta per ciascuno Quaderno si mette la partita . . ."

[31] Ibid. Chap. 34. *"E così sia saldo tutto il primo Quaderno con suo Giornale e Memoriale. E acciò sia più chiaro, di ditto saldo farai queſto altro scontro: cioè sommerai in un foglio tutte il dare del Quaderno croci e ponlo a man siniſtra, e sommerai tutto suo avere e ponlo a man deſtra; e poi queſte altre somme risommerai e farane di tutte quelle del dare una somma che si chiamerà summa summarium, e così farai una somma di tutte quelle dell'avere . . . Ora se queſte due summe summarium saranno pari . . . arguirai il tuo Quaderno essere ben guidato, tenuto e saldato . . . ; ma se l'una di ditte summe summarium avanzassel'altr a dinoterebbe errore nel tuo Quaderno. Il quale poi con diligenza converrà trovarlo con la induſtria dell'intelletto che Dio ti ha dato e con l'arteficio delle ragioni che avrai bene imparato."*

[32] Ibid. Chap. 33. *"Tutte queſte cose ordinatamente fatte e osservate, guarda non innovare più partita in alcun libro anziano al Quaderno, cioè in Memoriale e Giornale, perchè il saldo tutto di tutti i libri sempre si deve intendere fatto in un medesimo giorno."*

[33] Bariola. Part 2, p. 377.

[34] Vittorio Alfieri, *La partita doppia applicata alle scritture delle antiche aziende mercantili veneziane.*

[35] Manzoni, Domenico, *Quaderno doppio col suo giornale* (Venice, 1540), Part 1, chap. 1. *". . . libri principali, l'uno dimandato giornale, l'altro quaderno . . ."*

[36] Ibid. Part 1, chap. 6. *"Alcuni altri libretti particolarmente sono usitati, li quali mal si possono fare, imperochè sarebbe mal fatto che per ogni minima coscienza, di subito si prendesse li libri grandi con diligentia tenuti, . . . onde è coſtume fra mercanti praĉtici, di haver molti libri come ho detto, ne i quali si hanno a scrivere le cose menute che di giorno in giorno, et a hora per hora van facendo, uno de quali teniranno per scrivervi le spese menute che fanno per uso di casa, un altro per ponervi le spese de vila, et uno per spese di salariadi, ovvero per fabriche, o concieri de case, o de fitti, o d'intrade di terra ferma, . . . ne li quali libretti simplicemente si deve scrivere il tutto, il che, et come, quando, et dove, con li soi giorni, nomi, e cognomi, come di sopra al memorial fu detto, le qual cose, poi in capo d'un certo tempo, o di un mese, o d'una settimana che sia, di tutte quelle d'un medesimo libro in somma a uno per uno nel giornal si fa una partida, . . ."*

[37] Ibid. *Giornale,* entry No. 129.

[38] Ibid.

[39] Ibid. From the *Quaderno.*

[40] Ibid. Part 2, chap. 8. *"Un altro numero, nel principio davanti a ciascuna partida del giornale habbiamo poſto, oltra li doi che habbiamo detto disopra, il quale numero non opera cosa alcuna circa a l'ordine del quaderno, ma solamente è fatto per haver notitia del numero overo quantità de la partide di esso giornale, acciò di ciascuna secondo la varietà de soggetti, si possa averne separata cognitione. Et anche è fatto perchè ne renda più facili al ritrovar tal partide nel quaderno, si in dar a man manca come in haver a man deſtra, dove quelle scritte siano, imperochè, si come di una in una trahendola di giornale, le riponiamo in quaderno, così davanti a ciascuna in detto quaderno habbiamo poſto li medesimi numeri correspondenti alle medisime di esso giornale. Onde se con preſtezza voleſti ritrovar una partida del giornale, dove nel quaderno poſta fusse."*

[41] Beſta. Op. cit., vol. 3, p. 350.

[42] Manzoni. Op. cit., part 1, chap. 13.

[43] Ibid. Ledger account on page 8 of the *Quaderno.*

[44] Ibid. From the end of the *Quaderno.*

[45] Ibid. *Giornale,* entry No. 208.

[46] Ibid. *Giornale,* entry No. 216.

[47] Bariola. Op. cit., part 2, p. 378.

Besta. Op. cit., vol. 3, p. 381.
[48] Besta. Op. cit., vol. 3, p. 394.
Bariola. Op. cit., part 2, p. 380.
[49] Casanova, Alvise, *Specchio lucidissimo*, Venice, 1558, Introduction: "*Haverete etiam a intender questo, che il giornale è la radice del Libro et esso Libro è l'arbore, che tutta la sustantia del ditto Libro nasse dal ditto giornale, come dal suo generator . . .*"
[50] Ibid. From the *Giornal.*
[51] It was the usual practice during the Middle Ages to defray the cost of merchant vessels and divide the gains or losses among a group of investors. The risk factor was particularly potent in molding medieval commercial institutions. It was divided by means of *caratti*, or shares. At Genoa in the twelfth and thirteenth centuries, they were called *loca*. The usual investors in these shares were merchants who were actively engaged in overseas trade. Originally the skipper was also the ship owner, but with the rapid growth of commerce the skipper usually was just a shareholder. The number of shares usually varied from sixteen to seventy, and it was the general practice for the investors to provide, at their own expense, as many mariners for the vessel as the number of shares they owned. The largest vessels had a capacity of about 600 tons and they were manned by as many as 100 mariners.

Loca, says Professor Byrne, in ships of all sizes and types, were owned, bought and sold, pledged, hypothecated, given in *accomendatio* as freely in Genoa as merchandise of any sort. There were two ways of contracting for shipment of cargo: the merchants might agree to pay freight by weight, or they might lease or charter the entire vessel for a lump sum. To cover all the details of a shipment of goods, the merchant and the ship owners would go before the notary, who would carefully draw up a contract binding both parties. The typical contract consisted of three parts:

1. The obligation of the ship owners and the freight rates they charged the merchants.
2. The obligations of the merchants shipping the cargo.
3. Finally, the pledges and guarantees of both parties, with a statement of the penalties for failure to fulfill the terms of the contract.

(Eugenes H. Byrne, *Genoese Shipping in the Twelfth and Thirteenth Centuries*. Medieval Academy of America, 1930.)
[52] Casanova. Op. cit., from the *Giornal.*
[53] Ibid. From p. 55 of the *Libro.*
[54] Ibid. From end of the *Libro.*
[55] Bariola. Op cit., part 2, p. 374.
Besta. Op. cit., vol. 3, p. 380.
[56] Tagliente, Giovanni Antonio, *Luminario di arithmetica* (Venice, 1525). "*La regola del Quaderno, nota che la cosa debitora è sempre anciana alla cosa che die haver, et davanti le cosa che debitora se mete questo 'Per', e davanti la cosa che die haver se mete questo 'A', a nota che de una partida in Zornal se ne fa doi in libro una in dar e l'altra in haver. E sapi che 'l dar se mete in libro aman zancha e lo haver se mete in libro aman destra. Et lo giorno se mete in zornal de sopra la partida. Et in libro dentro la partida et anchor nota che le carte in Zornal se mete in capo la partida et nel libro le se mete nel ultimo da la partida. Et sapi che sempre el millesimo, se mete in libro de sopra la partida.*"
[57] Tagliente. Op. cit., *Luminario di arithmetica.*
[58] Bariola. Op. cit., part 2, p. 376.
[59] Bariola. Op cit., part 2, p. 379.

Chapter VI

THE SECOND CYCLE (1559 - 1795)

FTER 1559, double entry underwent a process of change which greatly increased its usefulness. There were factors tending to broaden the scope of accounting, such as the reorganization of public finance with the rise of nations after the fifteenth century, and the development of the technique of business administration incident to the growth of large enterprises, both profit-making and nonprofit-making. Changes in the methods of public finance did not result so much in improvement in the art of bookkeeping as in its adaptation to the needs of governments during the period of their expansion.

The emergence of large-scale business units did stimulate progress; double entry, having outgrown the bounds of the simple single-proprietorship, was then applied to this new kind of enterprise in which owner and management were no longer identical. Old mercantile bookkeeping was concerned only with changes in the owner's capital. New bookkeeping, called "patrimonial," still kept account of all changes in capital, but it's principal use was to account for what the capital produced and consumed. Before, the owner had personally operated his business and was interested only in knowing the amount of profit or loss; now, between the proprietor and the business there came a third person — an agent, a factor, or administrator, who operated the business and periodically submitted detailed reports to his superior of all expenses and income.

The literature of the period 1559–1795 reflects this change, but nowhere gives a complete and systematic exposition of it or of its accounting implications. There is a beginning of an accounting critique among the writers, and sporadically accounting theory appears, but this is all. Nowhere are these fragments woven into a consistent whole.

The comparative slowness of progress in accounting thought was due in part to Italy's loss of the commercial and political importance which she had possessed in the Renaissance period. With the discovery of the all-water route to the Orient, her primacy in commerce and banking passed to nations on the Atlantic Ocean. It was natural that the use of bookkeeping, the offshoot and auxiliary of commerce, should flourish in these new centers, while it became stagnant in Italy.

And so, the progress of double entry is now to be measured more by the extension of its use throughout Europe than by the development of the art itself. Knowledge of the system was made available by many translations of the best

Italian works of the first period and by original writings of authors of other nations, who however drew heavily from Italian treatises; there were Rogier, De Koninche, and Geestewelt in Holland; Hugh Oldcastle and Jack Peele in England; Martin Fustel in France; and Simon Stevin in Flanders. Europe was still learning to use the Italian method of double entry and did not seriously contest its leadership until late in the eighteenth century.

The procedure of bookkeeping, though undergoing some notable developments, did not develop in proportion to the vast changes which transformed all other fields of endeavor. Bookkeeping clung tenaciously to its antiquated forms, such as the long analytical journal and ledger entries in paragraph form, its cumbersome cross-index system, and the use of unnecessary technical phrases. Not until the nineteenth century, with the full impetus of the industrial revolution and a world trade freed at last from all feudal shackles and barriers, did double entry once more forge ahead and develop into what we know as modern accountancy. It is not surprising, therefore, that accounting literature makes few notable advances from 1559 to 1795, and contents itself with the expounding of principles and rules of procedure laid down long ago by Paciolo, Manzoni, and Casanova.[1]

DON ANGELO PIETRA

Pietra was a Benedictine monk. In 1586 he published at Mantua his *Indirizzo degli economi*, which deals with bookkeeping as applied to a monastery. He is the first author to think of a business enterprise as separate and distinct from its owner. This was by no means a new phenomenon. It had been inherent in the Florentine *compagnie* of the fourteenth and fifteenth centuries. It resulted from practical need, which during centuries gradually forced a distinction between the business entity and its owner.

Pietra's principal contribution to the literature of accounting is his interpretation of this fact. As seen by him, the central thesis of bookkeeping had shifted from the mere accounting for capital changes to an accounting for all changes affecting the financial status of a business. Pietra's importance may be better appreciated after a brief exposition of his system of double entry.[2]

Pietra describes three types of ledgers: (1) *libro di banco* (bank ledger), (2) *libro mercantesco* (mercantile ledger), and (3) *libro nobile* (noble ledger). The last is a financial or administrator's ledger, concerned principally with the income and expenses of capital investments which have no relation to the conduct of a mercantile or banking business — the type of ledger used by monasteries.[3]

Pietra's mechanics of bookkeeping are very similar to Casanova's. The *giornale* and the *libro doppio*, also named *libro maestro*, are the two principal books used. These are supplemented by numerous memorandum books, variously

called *memoriali*, *libretti*, *vacchette*, or *squarciafogli*, which are summarized at
the end of each month and entered in total in the journal.[4] The structure of the
journal entry is practically the same. The only difference is that the *Per*, meaning
"debit," appears only in the first entry at the top of the page and is not repeated
in subsequent entries on the same page. Another feature is the brevity of journal
entries. The long paragraph form characteristic of previous authors is now
beginning to disappear. An entry taken at random shows this: [5]

Adì 2 Giugno 1586

35 *D Mauro concelleraro // a Cassa, lire centotrenta, contegli per spendere,*
32 *come al mio libretto appare distintamente . . .*   *L. 130* ——

June 2, 1536

35 Debit D. Mauro concelleraro || credit cash 130 lire for expenses as
32 shown in the *libretto*   L. 130 ——

This is a debit to Father Mauro and a credit to cash for expenses, as shown in the
libretto. It is the second entry on the page; therefore, the *Per* preceding the debit
is missing.

There is hardly any difference at all in the ledger entry, though there is an
emphasizing of the title on the debit side of the account which is missing in
Casanova, and the totals of the accounts are placed directly under the money
amounts, instead of being placed in the middle of the accounts.

Pietra follows a slightly different procedure in balancing and closing the
ledger. The ledger was balanced once a year and, contrary to the tenets of earlier
authors, the same set of books was used if not yet filled.[6] The first step was to
compare all ledger entries with their journal entries for any possible mistakes.
This operation was called *puntare il libro*.[7] Following this, all nominal accounts
were closed into expenditure-and-income account (*spesa et entrata generale*).
The profit or loss realized was then closed into the capital account (*monastero
nostro*). Finally the capital and all other open accounts were closed into the
balance account (*esito generale di questo anno*). Pietra speaks of this account as a
trial balance, *summa summarium*, and says that if the debits and credits of this
account balanced, then the ledger was closed and correct.[8]

This *esito generale di quest'anno* is similar to Casanova's *resti di questo
libro*, and it serves as the basis for opening up the ledger for the new year. The
balance account of the old year is entered in the new year in the reverse order and
is called the *introito* account.[9] This procedure is exactly the same as Casanova's.
None of the accounts transferred or closed are journalized.

80

It was the rule of the Benedictine Order that the accounts of the monastery be reviewed by the abbot four times a year. Pietra, with keen insight, believes that this can be best accomplished by examination of detached statements reflecting the financial position of the institution. He maintains, however, that financial statements should be drawn up only once a year, when all annual income and expenses are known.[10] His statements are composed of three accounts taken bodily from the ledger: the *spesa et entrata generale* (i.e., the profit-and-loss account), the *monastero nostro* (i.e., the capital account, which he called the keystone of the whole ledger),[11] and the *esito generale di questo anno* (i.e., the balance account, containing all post-closing accounts). A close scrutiny of these three accounts is sufficient to acquaint one with the yearly financial operations of the monastery.[12] This is the first time that financial statements of any sort have been mentioned by an author, though such statements had been used by Florentines since the fourteenth century, as was shown in part I. Pietra's statements were mere crude beginnings, but nevertheless they represented the profit-and-loss statement, the balance-sheet, and a detailed statement of the capital of the monastery. These were advanced conceptions and were the direct result of segregating sharply the entity of the enterprise from its owner.

GRISOGONO SIMON

Grisogono, a native of Zara (Dalmatia), then within the Venetian domain, published at Venice in 1609 his book on double entry entitled *Il mercante arricchito dal perfetto quaderniere* (The merchant enriched by the perfect bookkeeper). It is a faithful reproduction of Casanova's book. Grisogono says in his introduction that his objective is to modernize Casanova's *Specchio lucidissimo*, but the changes he introduced are slight. He follows Manzoni in placing the preposition *A* before the credit titles of debit ledger entries, instead of the usual *Per* used by Casanova. Flori does the same thing in 1633. The best part of Grisogono's book is the complete set of double-entry books, with which he illustrates his text.[13]

GIOVANNI ANTONIO MOSCHETTI

In 1610, Giovanni Antonio Moschetti, a Venetian, published his book, *Dell'universal trattato di libri doppi*. He condemns the prevailing loose bookkeeping practices of his time and criticizes severely the ambiguous writings of his contemporaries.

Accounting critique seems to have made a start with Moschetti. He is among the first to allude to a system of single entry.[14]

His set of double-entry books was closely patterned on those of Manzoni and Casanova. From Manzoni he took over the cross-index system with its

81

consecutive numbers and the *inventario;* from Casanova he borrowed the method of closing and opening the ledger through the *resti di questo libro* account, and also the closing of all nominal accounts into profit and loss at the end of the year.

Moschetti introduces but one new feature, and this one innovation was dropped by subsequent writers: the two lines separating the debit from the credit in the journal entry are horizontal instead of vertical, as is shown in the following example: [15]

Adì ultimo detto

Finito l'anno si porterà il Pro e danno in cavedal a questo modo.

275   –   *per Pro e danno* === *A Cavedal di me Gio Antonio Moschetti del q*
    6   *sier Francesco d. 10712 g. 17 p. 12 porto in Cavedal per Saldo*
    2   *dell'anno presente*   *l. 1071 s. 5 g. 5, p. 12*

Date as above

At the end of the year the profit or loss is carried into capital
in the following manner.

275   –   Debit profit and loss === credit my capital Gio. Antonio Moschetti
    6   q. ser Francesco for d. 10712, g. 12. p. 12, which is carried into capital,
    2   thus closing the profit-and-loss account of the present year.
                                        l. 1071, s. 5, g. 5, p. 12

This is a debit to profit and loss, and a credit to capital for the profit made during the year.

MATTEO MAINARDI

Mainardi, a Bolognese, published at Bologna in 1632 his work, *La scrittura mercantile formalmente regolata.* It is a pamphlet of only 34 pages, and double entry is described without a word of theory. It is merely a long example of a set of books, far inferior to those produced by Venetian writers.[16]

LUDOVICO FLORI

Flori, a Jesuit, wrote his *Trattato del modo di tenere il libro doppio domestico* for the benefit of Sicilian monasteries and published it in Palermo in 1633. It is an outstanding work. Flori's precise and clear-cut definitions and his illustrations of double-entry books testify to his firm grasp of the subject of bookkeeping.

He was well acquainted with the writings of previous authors, whom he divides into two groups: writers of mercantile bookkeeping, such as Paciolo,

Casanova, Manzoni, Tagliente, Moschetti, Grisogono, and others; and writers of administrative bookkeeping (*libri nobili*), such as Simon Stevin and Don Angelo Pietra. He believes Pietra's work is of such a high order that it cannot be improved upon, but he is induced to write his book because Pietra's work was unknown in Sicily.[17] He naturally follows Pietra very closely, but his more detailed and careful elucidation of bookkeeping principles and technique distinguishes his book as a masterpiece in its own right.

In his introduction, Flori says that, although several systems of bookkeeping have been developed by the ancients, only double entry, which had its origin in mercantile transactions and trade, reached perfection. He tells how gradually it came into use by enterprises of a nonmercantile nature, such as hospitals, religious orders, government, and family economy.[18] It is evident that Flori was fully aware of the advancement made in bookkeeping. His contribution was responsible for a large share of it. With Pietra and Flori, the literature of bookkeeping takes cognizance of the expansion of double entry beyond the orbit of the mercantile firm and the emergence of the entity of the enterprise as distinctly separated from its one or more owners.

Flori, in his introduction, also states the object of his work: to write and arrange his book so clearly that one could easily trace the course of transactions through the accounts and also learn how income and expenses are properly allocated to the fiscal periods in which they arose. The ledger, he said, should be kept up to date so that information on the financial status of the monastery would always be available.[19]

This is the first time that an author mentions the placing of transactions in their proper fiscal periods; Flori makes it one of the principal points of his book. This is a great advance and shows Flori's deep understanding of bookkeeping.

Flori uses the customary set of books, the *giornale* and the *libro doppio*, supplemented by numerous memorandum books, which are called by him *libri semplici*, or single books, in contrast to the ledger, which is called *libro doppio*, or double book. The ledger was on a double-entry basis, whereas memorandum books did not necessarily distinguish between debits and credits, but merely listed in an informal manner information necessary for journal entries.

Flori's definitions are interesting: He defines the journal as a book in which are entered daily all transactions relative to accounts kept in the ledger.[20] He is careful to distinguish between an entry and an account. An entry, he explains, is the statement of a sum of money or things owed by one to someone else, with its proper explanation, written once in the journal and twice in the ledger, as a debit and as a credit.[21] A ledger account is composed of one or more entries, both debit and credit, relating to a particular person or thing.[22]

Flori follows Pietra's lead in classifying transactions into three groups.

1. Cash transactions (*imborsa e sborsa denari per cosa venduta e comprata*).
2. Credit transactions (*quando si compra o vende a credenza*).
3. Bank transactions (*questa è la cessione*).[23]

This classification includes all entries arising from active trading. He goes on then to describe journal entries in great detail. Four things are necessary to set up journal entries: 1. the debtor, 2. the creditor, 3. the sum owed, and 4. the reason why it is owed. The amount is always figured at the end on the abacus,[24] which was essential for computing all operations of arithmetic.

Flori departs from the usual prepositions, *Per* and *A*, meaning "for" and "to," and uses instead *da* and *A*, meaning "from" and "to." He believes that *da* is more logical than *Per*, though he omits it completely from the journal and uses it only in the ledger.[25] A journal entry with its postings in the ledger will illustrate this.[26]

+ *Prim. Ind. // 1633*

A 2 di Gennaro. —

r   8   *Calzoleria // alla Cassa* ____ *una e tt. 6 oer una mezina di sola*

r   12   (1.6 —

January 2, 1633

r   8   Debit shoe store | | credit cash for one onza and 6 tari for leather

r   12   1.6 —

The preposition *Da*, which stands for debit, is omitted from journal entries. Only the preposition *A*, *alla* in this case, is used. The two *r*'s to the left of the entry are the tick marks used by Flori when checking the journal against the ledger. The two symbols, ‾(and *tt*, indicate monetary units, in this case onze and tari. One *onza* was equivalent to 30 tari, and each of these to 20 grani. This was one of the monetary systems used in Sicily during the seventeenth century. The two vertical lines, says Flori, serve only to separate the debit from the credit and to indicate that, for every journal entry, two entries must be made in the ledger; one a debit and the other a credit.[27] The debit entry in the ledger is as follows:[28]

r   *Calzoleria dare a dì 2 Gennaro* ____ *1.6 Contanti per una mezina di*

Suola vagliono per la Cassa   12   1.6

84

Debit shoe store on January 2, for onze 1.6 for leather, as shown in cash on p. 12 _____ 1.6

The credit entry to the cash account: [29]

r   *Havere a 2 dì Gennaro* ____ *1.6 dalla Calzoleria.* ____ 8 1.6 __
((

r   Credit cash on January 2, for onze 1.6 and debit shoe store on page 8
_____ 1.6

These two ledger entries are self-explanatory. The preposition *Da*, or *Dalla*, is used in the credit entry where the contra debit account is mentioned. This procedure is followed in all credit entries.

There is no change in the cross-index system. In the journal the usual fraction appears, and in the ledger the two entries are cross-referenced with the two accounts with no mention of the journal page number.

Flori follows up Simon Stevin's "compound entry" (*partita collettiva*). When a transaction involves more than two parties or accounts, only one journal entry is made, a compound entry, instead of the earlier practice of splitting transactions into as many journal entries as there were elements in the transaction.[30] The modern tendency to classify and synthesize financial data already has begun to make itself felt. An example will show how far Flori differs from his predecessors in this respect: [31]

+ *Prim. Ind. // 1633*
A 30. di Aprile

r 16   *Salarij diversi // alli appresso* ____ *sedici, se li fan buoni anticipata-*
r   0   (
       mente per l'ultimo terzo dell'anno presente prima Ind. et a compimento, etc. degl' infrascritti loro salarij, come medico, barbiero, avvocato, procuratore, e sollecitatorer espettivamente di questo nostro collegio, cioè A.

r 16   *Dottor Carlo Segni nostro Medico*_____ 4 _____
                               (

r 16   *M. Francesco Nigno nostro barbiero*_____ 2 _____
                               (

r 17   *Dott. Horatio Archinto nostro Avvocato*_____ 4 _____
                               (

r 17   *Domenico Tagliavia nostro Procuratore*_____ 4 _____
                               (

r 17 *Raffaele Botti nostro Sollecitatore*_____ 2 _____

(—

___ 16   16 ____

(

April 30, 1633

r 16 Debit salaries | |Credit the following people for 16 onze for the last
r   0   third of the present year, etc. The salaries are for the doctor, barber,
        lawyer, attorney, and solicitor of this monastery, Credit:

r 16 Doctor Carlo Segni, our doctor_____ 4 _____

(

r 16 M. Francesco Nigno, our barber_____ 2 _____

(

r 17 Doctor Horatio Archinto, our lawyer_____ 4 _____

(

r 17 Domenico Tagliavia, our attorney_____ 4 _____

(

r 17 Raffaele Botti, our solicitor_____ 2 _____

(

—

___ 16   16 ____

(

The construction of the entry differs somewhat from the usual form encountered
so far. The five credits, instead of following the debit immediately, are set down
underneath one another at the end of the entry. The phrase *alli appresso* means
"to the following" and refers to the credits listed underneath. The cross-indexing
is a little different also. The zero in the denominator of the fraction means that
the credits are more than one and that they are listed separately below. Each of
the credits has the ledger folio number at the left of the entry.

The method of cross-indexing the ledger is exactly the same as that used
in all previous ledgers, with the exception of one peculiarity caused by compound
entries. Referring to the example cited, the debit to the salary account would
have to bear the page number of the five credit accounts. Flori overcomes this
difficulty by referring the reader to the journal for the page number of the credit
accounts. Strangely enough, he does not give the journal page, but writes a
double zero in the place of the ledger folio to indicate the existence of several
credits. The reader has to trace the journal entry by means of the date. The debit
entry in the salary account clarifies this peculiarity: [32]

+ 1. Ind. // 1633

r   *Salarij diversi dare a dì primo di Maggio* ____ 16.

(

*alli detti, per l'ultimo terzo come in Giornale.*_____ 00 16 _____

(

1633

r   Debit salaries on May 1st for 16 onze, and credit several persons for the
last third, as is shown in the journal_____ page oo ____ 16 __
                                                                 (

Flori also differs from Pietra in the matter of which entries are to be
journalized. He believes that nothing should be entered in the ledger which is
not first entered in the journal. The only exceptions he allows are the carrying
forward of accounts from one page to another and the correction of errors made
in the ledger, which he justifies on the ground that no new transactions have
arisen.[33]

Flori's outline of a crude petty-cash system is also of interest. It is much
nearer to modern practice than Paciolo's *spese di casa*, which is nothing more
than a cash allowance for household expenses. Flori, instead, says that small cash
funds are intrusted and charged to the accounts of the Fathers, who have to
meet petty cash expenses. When the fund is exhausted, they give an account of
their expenses to the *P. Procuratore* (administrative head and bookkeeper of the
convent), who gives them credit. The entries are, as Flori says, a debit to
Fathers to whom are intrusted petty cash funds and a credit to cash for the
amount of the funds. When the funds are exhausted, the expenses for which they
were used are debited and the Fathers are credited, thus eliminating the Fathers'
liabilities for the petty cash entrusted to them.[34]

The first mention of a suspense account (*conto pendente*) is found in Flori's
book. He defines it as an account in which are temporarily placed all entries
whose true nature is not known at the time. The purpose of the account is to
avoid keeping the books open too long while trying to determine the nature of
the transactions in doubt.[35]

The ledger, called both *libro doppio* and *libro maestro*, is defined as the book
in which are entered, by means of the journal, in an orderly and regular fashion,
all that goes in and out of the enterprise.[36] The ledger is called *libro maestro*
(master book), because it is the principal record and summarizes all the other
bookkeeping records.[37] By the skillful use of definitions, Flori shows the inter-
dependence of books of account. Even though the ledger is the principal
bookkeeping record, its importance is dependent upon the records which gather
its data.

Following Pietra's suggestion, Flori groups all ledgers into three categories:
bankers' ledgers (*libro de banchieri*); merchants' ledgers (*libro de' mercanti*); and
domestic ledgers (*libro domestico o nobile*). The last named was used by those
who live on the interest of their capital investments and was the type of ledger
used by monasteries.[38]

Flori also groups all accounts into four major classes: 1. Assets accounts (i.e., *conti, e rubriche, che formano l'Entrata; come massarie, possessioni, territorij, vigne, etc.*); 2. Nominal accounts (i. e., *conti che formano la spesa, come spesa ordinaria, vettovaglie consumate quest'anno, frutti di rendite, etc.*); 3. Merchandise accounts (i.e., *conti delle officine: come cantine, granari, cassa, etc.*); and 4. Customers and creditors accounts (i.e., *debitori e creditori*). In this last group, Flori also includes the profit-and-loss account (*spesa e entrata generale*), the balance account (*l'esito*), and the capital account (*collegio nostro*).[39]

Flori was the first author to give such an extensive classification of accounts. Pietra deserves credit for making a beginning, but Flori's work was far more systematic and complete.

His method of balancing and closing the ledger is exactly the same as Pietra's. First of all, the journal must be checked against the ledger (*puntare il libro*).[40] Flori uses the letter *r* as his tick mark. This checking was to be done not once a year, but as often as possible. He mentions that the Bank of Palermo checked all its entries daily. In other types of enterprises, he suggests that it be done at least every four months.[41]

It is necessary at this point, Flori says, to draw up the *bilancio del libro* (the trial balance), and he goes into a lengthy discussion explaining it. He defines it as a brief summary of the balances of open accounts, in which the total debits and credits are reduced to equality.[42] He proceeds to explain that there are two kinds of *bilanci*. One of them is a plain trial balance, drawn up at any time of the year with no particular thought as to form, but merely as a means of checking the correctness of the ledger and affording a quick glance at the financial position of the monastery. The true *bilancio*, approximating the modern work sheet, is made at the end of the year, when the ledger is balanced and closed.[43] No entry is to be made on the books until it is completed and correct. This *bilancio* is drawn up on a separate sheet of paper and is divided into two distinct sections, one for expenditures and income (*spesa et entrata generale*), and the other for the balance-sheet items (*l'esito*). The expenditure-and-income section is first totaled and its balance transferred to capital (*collegio nostro*). The balance of the capital in turn is entered into the *esito* section of the *bilancio* which, if correct, should now balance. The *bilancio* is then entered in the journal and posted to the ledger. With this, the ledger is completely closed. Finally the *esito* account is reversed to open up the ledger for the new year.

It is clear that Flori uses this *bilancio*, or trial balance, not only to prove the correctness of the ledger, but to facilitate its closing, which is one of the purposes of the modern work sheet. Flori was the first to distinguish between the trial balance and the *esito* account. He defines the *esito* as an account in which are entered at the end of every year the balances of the remaining accounts after all nominal accounts are closed. [44] He also recognizes the *esito* account not only as a balance account, but as a statement showing the financial position of the monastery: a comparison of one *esito* account with that of the previous year shows the changes in the financial position. [45] This is conclusive proof that Flori knew the significance of a financial statement. Like Pietra, he says it is sufficient to submit the *spesa et entrata generale* (expenditure-and-income account) and the *esito di quest'anno* (balance-sheet of the present year) to the superiors of the monastery for the review of the institution's affairs. He makes use of them as two separate statements and not merely as two accounts of the ledger.

Flori also was the first to distinguish between the trial balance, ledger closing, and financial statements. His precise definitions, his profound knowledge and very detailed elucidation of bookkeeping principles and mechanics, all contributed to make his book the highest expression of early bookkeeping. One has to reach the nineteenth century to find another author of Flori's calibre.

GIOVANNI DOMENICO PERI

Peri's book, *Il negoziante*, published at Genoa in 1636, deals wholly with commercial customs and practices, and only incidentally with bookkeeping. Only nine pages of a voluminous book are dedicated to double entry.

Peri says that the merchants should keep two books: the *giornale* or *manuale* and the *libro*. He then explains in a very summary fashion how journal and ledger entries are constructed. His only innovation is to change *Per* and *A* to *Tale per* and *Vanno per*, which were never adopted by anyone else. An example of a journal entry [46] is shown below:

+ *1637, a dì 2, di Genaro*

2
—
3   *Cassa a mio carico per Lir. 100,000 moneta corrente, che sono in essa vanno per il mio Pietra Ventura conto proprio.*   *l. 100,000*

January 2, 1637

2
—
3   Debit cash for Lire 100,000 and credit Pietra Ventura   l. 100,000

In the ledger the same phrases are used, as shown by the following debit entry: [47]

1637 a 2 dì Genaro

Cassa a carico del nostro Pietro, per esso; vanno per conto proprio 3.   *l. 100,000*

January 2, 1637

Debit cash and credit Pietro, on page 3   l. 100,000

89

Credit entry: [48]

Pietro mio conto proprio
Havere 1637 a 2 di genaro in quanto importano li contanti, che sono in Cassa
vanno in essa 2.   *l. 100,000*

Credit Pietro on January 2, 1637, and debit cash on p. 2.   l. 100,000

This summarizes all that Peri had to say about bookkeeping. Needless to say his book is of little importance.

BASTIANO VENTURI

Of greater interest is the publication of Venturi's *Scrittura conteggiante di possessioni* in 1655. Like Flori, Venturi writes about the domestic ledger. He is the first to segregate the cash account from the ledger. Cash is set up in the journal by the addition of two columns, one entitled "receipts" and the other "disbursements." This arrangement saves postings to the cash account. To balance the ledger, the cash balance in the journal has to be inclosed. For this reason this system was nick-named "the lame system of double entry" (*scrittura doppia a partite zoppe*). [49]

Venturi launched a vigorous attack on the excessive technicality of bookkeeping phraseology, whose meaning was unknown to laymen. It is evident that criticism, both negative and constructive, was gathering momentum. Soon controversies began which were to lay the groundwork for the development of future theories.

GIACOMO VENTUROLI

The Bolognese priest Giacomo Venturoli published his *Scorta d'economia* in 1666, in which he explained the system of double entry by means of a dialogue between father and son. He adopted Bastiano Venturi as his model and followed him throughout, contributing nothing to bookkeeping. [50]

ANTONIO ZAMBELLI

Zambelli, who in 1671 published at Milan his *Mercantesche dichiarazioni della scrittura doppia*, carried the critique a step further than Venturi did. He raised the whole question of the impersonality of accounts, combatted the use of the ledger without the journal, and sought to distinguish between private accounts and open accounts. His whole book is devoted to appraising and criticizing bookkeeping practices. [51]

ONOFRIO SBERNIA PUGLIESI

In the same year Pugliesi's *Prattica economica numerale* appeared at Palermo. There is nothing original in this book: Pugliesi slavishly followed Flori's work and at times copied it exactly.

LODOVICO CORTICELLI

Of very little substance is Corticelli's *Mastro di casa famigliare*, which appeared at Bologna in 1696. It is a book of only thirty-nine pages and is chiefly concerned with the laborers' payroll — how best to insure its accuracy and eliminate all possibilities of defrauding the workers. [52]

GIACOMO DELLA GATTA

Half a century passed without a writer of note, but in 1744 Della Gatta published at Milan his *Nuova practica di arithmetica mercantile* in which he discussed the application of double entry to all types of enterprises and also described the system of single entry. He advocates use of the profit-and-loss account (*avanzi e disavanzi*). [53]

BALUGANI PELLEGRINO

More than one hundred and fifty years after the appearance of Pietra's work, Pellegrino still considers it of such value that he acknowledges it as his model. In fact his *Instruzione brevissima*, which appeared at Modena in 1745, is a faithful reproduction of the *Indrizzo degli economi*. The fact that Pellegrino goes back a century and a half to copy the work of an eminent but nevertheless antiquated author, shows to what level Italian bookkeeping literature and practice had fallen during the eighteenth century.

TOMASO DOMENICO BREGLIA

In 1751 Breglia published at Naples his *Trattato di scrittura doppia baronale*. On the whole he follows Flori's system of bookkeeping. The best part of his work is a complete set of books for a large baronial estate. However, no advance is made in bookkeeping. [54]

PIETRO PAOLO SCALI

Scali's *Trattato del modo di tenere la scrittura dei mercanti* appeared at Leghorn in 1755. Scali introduces nothing new except his division of ledger accounts into three general groups, [55] as follows:

> *Conti propri*, accounts not held with persons;
> *Effetti in natura*, all merchandise accounts; and
> *Corrispondenti*, accounts with people with whom business is transacted.

Scali explains his system by the method of questions and answers.

GUISEPPE FORNI

Forni published his *Trattato teorico-pratico della vera scrittura doppia* at Pavia in 1790. He was the first person to apply himself seriously to the development of a theory of double entry. His theory, however, is elementary and he spends most of his time in making an analysis of the *bilancio consuntivo* (summary balance), which he would substitute for the *spesa et entrata generale*. Like Scali, he sets forth his theory by means of questions and answers.

On the practical side, he draws up a complete ledger (*mastro*), without the journal. It is constructed in exactly the same manner as those of his predecessors. The only development is in his theoretical exposition.

CONCLUSION

No theory of accounting was devised from the time of Paciolo down to the opening of the nineteenth century. Suggestions of theory appear here and there, but not to the extent necessary to place accountancy on a systematic basis. The reason is obvious. Authors were not interested in ascertaining the nature of accounts and their relationship or in formulating general laws which would coördinate the whole of double entry. They were chiefly engaged in the solution of practical problems and in gathering examples to demonstrate how entries should be made in the books. The result was that, instead of a gradual formation of a body of theory, which might have organized and explained the principles of double entry, there grew up instead a great mass of rules applicable to particular cases.

NOTES

[1] Bariola. Op. cit., part 2, chaps. 14, 15, 16.
   G. Brambilla. Op. cit., p. 82.
[2] Bariola. Op. cit., part 2, pp. 405–410.
   Besta. Op. cit., vol. 3, p. 396.
[3] Pietra, Angelo. *Indirizzo degli economi* (Mantova, 1586), chap. 5. "*Lasciando dunque da parte i primi due soprascritti Libri doppi, cioè banchiere e mercantesco, i quali non fanno al nostro proposito; dico che'l libre nobile . . . è quello che si come è necessario a tutti gli cittadini, nobili e titolati, che vivono delle proprie rendite; ugualmente ha da servire a i Monasteri . . . che desiderano tenere la scrittura regolata; nel quale con buonissimo ordine s'hanno da notare giornalmente l'entrate, le spese, i granari, le cantine, con li debitori, e i creditori del Monastero . . .*"
[4] Ibid. Chap. 17. "*. . . et questa servirà come memoriale per saper mettere le partite a giornale nel fine del mese . . .*"
[5] Ibid. From the *Giornale*.
[6] Ibid. Chap. 30. "*. . . prima è da avvertire, che quantunque un Libro maestro possa servire ad un anno solo, nondimeno per l'uso si comprende, che non dovendo esso Libro haver meno di carte 500, molto pochi o nessuno Monastero lo cambia ogni anno, ma per non molti-*

plicare spesa e copia di libri senza alcuno giovamento, se ne servono quattro o cinque anni più e meno, secondo la quantità e qualità dell'entrata; se bene ogn' anno lo saldano con l istesso ordine e solennità . . ."

[7] Ibid. Chap. 52. *"Per gli errori, che di giorno in giorno si possano commettere in danno del Monastero dee, il sollecito ragionato o computista, almeno due o tre volte l'anno puntare il suo Libro; ma avanti che si ponga a fare il bilancio nel fine dell'anno cotal puntamento gli è al tutto necessario."*

[8] Ibid. Chap. 58. *"Et per l'ultima diligenza di questo tuo Libro punterai finalmente tutte le partite composte doppo che lo puntasti, che riferiscono tanto all'esito quanto alla spesa e all'entrata generale e al Monastero nostro; e come compendio e conclusione di tutto il Libro maestro."*

[9] Ibid. Chap. 30. *". . . scriverai l'introito di esso senza metterlo al Giornale, il quale Introito non è altro che un principal fondamento d'esso Libro Maestro, e lo potrai copiare dall'Esito del Libro antecedente scrivendolo al contrario; poi che l'esito è scritto debitore, all'Introito si fa creditore e dove è scritto creditore all'Introito si fa debitore . . ."*

[10] Ibid. Chap. 60. *"Se bene per le ordinationi della nostra Congregatione si comanda che'l Padre Celleraro quattro fiate l'anno dia i conti del suo maneggio al Reverendo Padra Abate, in presenza degli altri Padri Decani del Monastero, tuttavia non ha dubbio alcuno che questi tali conti non si possono dare realmente e perfettamente (per quel che a me ne paia) sol perchè nel fine dell'anno, quando compitamente si fa la spesa e l'entrata havuta, . . ."*

[11] Ibid. Chap. 30. *". . . e ancor la partita del Monastero nostro, la quale è quella che non solamente salda l'introito e l'esito, ma è come chiave e sugello di tutto il Libro Doppio."*

[12] Ibid. Chap. 60. *". . . havendo l'occhio solamente alla spesa e all'entrata generale e all'esito et alla partita del Monastero nostro, si vedono compendiosamente le facende di tutto l'anno intero, e ritrovando le stesse officine nelle carte citate, si vede tanto distintamente il quare e il quia che non vi può restare luogo da dubitare."*

[13] Simon, Grisogono. *Il mercante arricchito dal perfetto quaderniere* (Venetia, Vecchi, 1609).

Bariola. Op. cit., part 2, p. 422.

Besta. Op. cit., vol. 3, p. 400.

[14] Moschetti, Giovanni Antonio. *Dell'universal trattato di libri doppi* (Venetia, Luca Valentini, 1610), book 1, p. 5. *". . . alcuni . . . per non saper bene i termini del quaderno, confonder la scrittura doppia con la ugnola, come posso affermar d'haver veduto io in molti . . ."*

[15] Ibid. Book 2, p. 102.

[16] Bariola. Op. cit., part 2, p. 423.

Besta. Op. cit., vol. 3, p. 402.

[17] Flori, *Il libro doppio domestico* (Palermo, 1667). Proemio, p. 1. *". . . vi erano alcuni libri in Stampa, che pienamente trattavano di questa materia. Perchè tralasciando quei, che spettano a mercanti scritti, e mandati in luce da Fr. Luca dal Borzo, Luigi Casanova, Domenico Manzoni, Gio. Tagliente, Gio. Antonio Moschetti, Simon Grisogono, e altri; e quelli ancora, che hanno scritto, o' per dir meglio, accennato solamente il modo di tenere i libri Nobili, e di gran maneggio, come Simone Stevino in un suo trattato, che intitolò Apologistica Principum; Sapeva, che il molto Reverendo Padre D. Angelo Pietra Monaco di San Benedetto nel suo libro, che intitolò Indrizzo de gl'Economi, ne trattava così bene, e con tanta distintione, che a mio giudizio non si può avanzare . . . Ma perchè poi mi sono accorto che . . . la detta opera . . . è da pochi ch'io sappia, o forse da niuno in questi paesi usata . . . mi son risoluto . . . a scrivere quello, ch'io stesso ho osservato circa l'esatezza, e diligenza del detto Autore in questa materia: e dichiarando al meglio, che mi sarà possibile con gli esempi delle cose nostre molte delle cose dette da lui . . ."*

[18] Ibid. Proemio, page 3. *"Per tener bene adunque la Scrittura e i libri de' conti sono stati da i nostri Antichi in diversi tempi trovati, e inventati diversi modi, ma niuno di essi ha giamai potuto arrivare alla perfettione di quello che si serve del Libro Doppio; col quale non solamente si consequisce perfettissimamente il suddetto fine, che si pretende, ma ancora, s'è ben tenuto, e come si conviene, acquista da quello la Scrittura appresso di tutti indubitata fede, la quale*

ancora vien confermata con publica autorità appresso tutte le Nationi. Che perciò tutti i mercanti, e negotianti del mondo, quando vogliono che alli suoi libri si presti intiera fede, non si servono d'altro modo, che del Libro Doppio. Il quale se bene hebbe la sua origine da i negotij, e traffichi mercantili; si è steso però col tempo ancora alle faccende domestiche, con tanta esatezza, e perfettione serve all' Economica . . ."

[19] Ibid. Proemio, page 4. *". . . che questo Libro sia talmente ordinato e disposto, che in esso, non solamente si veda praticamente il modo di formar qualsivoglia partita occorente in giornale, e di riferirla a Libro in modo, che sempre si tenga il libro bilanciato; ma ancora vi si ordini, e disponga la scrittura di maniera, che ciascun' anno habbia con la sua spesa il credito ancora della sua propria entrata, e si tengono talmente tutti i conti lesti, che in ogni tempo si possa vedere facilmente con chiarezza, e distintione tutto lo stato di ciascuna casa o' collegio, e renderne, quando bisognerà, esatissimo conto, etiandio in assenza di quello, che tiene il libro. E questo è lo scopo e fine principale di questa instruttione . . ."*

[20] Ibid. Part 1, p. 6. *"Giornale la prima cosa è un libro nel quale si scrivono giornalmente le partite, che indifferentemente occorrono appartenenti a i conti, che si tengono nel Libro."*

[21] Ibid. Part 1, p. 6. *"Partita non è altro, che una somma di denari, o di robba dovuta da qualch' uno ad un'altro con la sua dichiaratione, scritta una volta nel giornale, e due volte nel Libro, una in debito e l'altra in credito di qualche conto."*

[22] Ibid. Part 1, p. 6. *"Conto è una, o più partite nel Libro spettanti a qualche persona particolare, o a qualche cosa surrogata scrittagli a debito, o a credito."*

[23] Ibid. Part 1, p. 16.

[24] Ibid. Part 1, p. 12. *"Nel formare qualsivoglia partita in Giornale si devono esprimere necessariamente quattro cose, cioè il Debitore, il creditore, la somma, che si deve, e la causa perchè si deve: e poi tirar fuori la detta somma in abaco."*

[25] Ibid. Part 1, p. 31. *"Mi resta per compimento del Giornale, a dire qualche cosa de' due termini, Per, e A, o come altri vogliono, Per, e In, usati da molti così nel Giornale, come nel Libro . . . Hor mentre, che io stavo cōponendo il nostro esemplare m'è souvenuto un altro modo d'usare in parte questi termini, e in parte mutarli per la ragione, che dirò appresso. Ritenendo dunque l'A, per connotativo di credito, e indice del creditore, piglio il Da, per l'altro termine, che dinota debito, e mostra, chi sia il Debitore. E di questo se bene io non mi servo nel Giornale, tuttavia, chi volesse, se ne può servire con più ragione, com'io stimo, che non si servono i primi del Per; perchè mettendosi questo termine Da, overo facendo, che s'intenda posto avanti il Debitore di qualsivoglia partita in Giornale, s'intende secondo ogni buono, e regolato modo di parlare, che Dal tal Debitore si deve al tal Creditore la tal somma, etc. Cosa che non riesce così bene servendosi del Per."*

[26] Ibid. The *Giornale*, p. 3.

[27] Ibid. Part 1, p. 15. *"Quelle due lineette poi // non servono per altro se non per distinguere il Debitore dal Creditore: E per accennare, che d'ogni partita scritta nel Giornale se ne devono far due a Libro, cioè una in debito al conto del Debitore, e una in credito al conto del Creditore."*

[28] Ibid. The *Libro Doppio*, p. 8.

[29] Ibid. *Libro Doppio*, p. 12.

[30] Ibid. Part I, p. 22. *"Partita Colletiva adunque è quella, che, scrivendosi nel Giornale una volta sola, e comprendendo in se molte altre partite per la medesima causa, si riporta al Libro alcune volte, una volta a conto del Debitore, e due, o più volte a conto di diversi creditori: altre volte, due, e più volte a conto di diversi debitori, e una volta a conto del creditore. Il che si fa in questa maniera, e per la seguente ragione.*

"Occorre spesse volte, che vi saranno molti debitori, che dovranno ad un creditore alcune somme per la medesima causa: overo si troverà un debitore, che dovrà alcune somme a diversi creditori, pure per la medesima causa. In questo capo procedendo alla semplice, si dovrebbono formare in Giornale tante partite distinte, quanti sono li debiti, e le somme, che si devono, replicando tante volte il nome del debitore, o creditore quanti sono li debitori, o creditori. Hora per fuggir questo travaglio, e per abbreviar la scrittura, si suol formare di tutti solamente una partita . . ."

[31] Ibid. The *Giornale*, p. 12.

[32] Ibid. The *Libro Doppio*, p. 16.

[33] Ibid. Part 2, pp. 89–90. *"Il P.D. Angelo Pietra nel cap. 42 dice, che se bene il Giornale è onninamente necessario al Libro Doppio, nondimono vi sono le seguenti partite, le quali, o si trasportano dal Libro Vecchio al nuovo, o in esso giornalmente, o al fin dell'anno si formano senza metterle in Giornale . . .*

"Nondimeno noi incliniamo più al contrario, e giudichiamo assolutamente, che nel Giornale si debbano scrivere tutte le suddette partite, fuorchè i saldi, che si tirano dall' una carta all'altra (perchè in questi non si fa nuova partita, ma si continua solamente il medesimo Conto, in altro foglio) e tutti quelli Storni, che si fanno per emendar gl'errori fatti solamente nel Libro . . . e finalmente l'Esito dell'anno presente, e Introito del seguente, quando il Libro nonsi muta, . . ."

[34] Ibid. Part 2, p. 72. *"Si avvete di più, che da questo conto di Cassa ne nascono alcuni altri, che sono come tante altre casse, o come dependenti dalla prima. E questi sono i conti de gl'officiali subordinati, a i quali il P. Procuratore somministra denari per spendere, a ciascuno secondo l'offitio suo, e poi a suoi tempi ne piglia conto. E quando li da denari, ne da credito alla cassa, e debito a i detti offitiali, e quando ne piglia conto, da debito della spesa alle officine, e a i conti, a i quali spetta, e credito alli detti offitiali, i quali d'ordine del P. Procuratore spesse volte esigono qualche somma da qualche debitore, o pagano qualche creditore. E quando rendono conto di queste somme riscosse, o pagate, se ne da debito, o credito ad essi offitiali, e credito o debito a detti debitori o creditori."*

[35] Ibid. Part 2, p. 70. *"Conti Pendenti è un conto dove si scrive tutto quello ch'entra, o esce senza sapere di certo per all'hora a chi si habbia d'applicare in particolare quell' Entrata, o quella Spesa. E. questo conto serve per non tener fra tanto sospesa la Scrittura."*

[36] Ibid. Part 1, p. 5. *"Il Libro doppio si può descrivere in questa maniera, cioè Libro Doppio, o vero Maestro (come altri il chiamano) è quello nel quale per mezzo del suo Giornale si scrive ordinata, e regolatamente tutto quello, che secondo il grado, e la professione di ciascuno, entra, e esce, e tutti i debiti, e crediti di qualsivoglia persona, o altra cosa surrogata, con le quali si tenga conto."*

[37] Ibid. Part 1, p. 6. *"Si chiama ancora Libro Maestro."*

[38] Ibid. Part 1, p. 7. *"Il Libro de' Banchieri (Appresso de quali per esser persone publiche, e giuridiche molti depositano i lor denari) è quello nel quale non si scrivono altri conti, se non quello della Cassa con li creditori, e debitori . . . Il Libro de' Mercanti è quello dove si scrivono i Capitali, le mercantie, e tutti i conti, che nel negotiare apportano Utile, o Danno, col conto della Cassa, Debitori, e Creditori. Il Domestico finalmente, o Nobile, come altri lo chiamano, è quello, del quale si servono quei, che vivono delle proprie entrate, i quali senza tenere in deposito denari, o robe d'altri; e senza essercitar veruna Sorte di mercantie, scrivono in esso solamente i conti dell'entrata, che hanno, e delle spese, che fanno, il conto di Cassa con li Debitori, e Creditori, che giornalmente si creano . . . E di questo terzo Libro s'hanno a servire i Religiosi per tenere i loro conti."*

[39] Ibid. Part 2, p. 49.

[40] Ibid. Part 2, p. 97. *"Il puntare il Libro non è altro, che riconoscere se tutte le partite scritte si confrontino, e mettervi qualche segno, emendati e corretti prima gli errori che vi fussero."*

[41] Ibid. Part 2, p. 98. *"In quanto al tempo di puntare la scrittura, si dice che quanto più spesso si fa, meglio è. I Libri grandi, numerosi, e frequentati, come sono quei della Tavola di Palermo, si puntano ogni giorno. Gl'altri minori, se si puntano ogni mese, sarebbe bene, pure chi non potesse, lo può fare quando vuole. Noi usiamo puntar la nostra scrittura almeno ogni quattro mesi, cioè al fine d'Aprile, d'Agosto, e Dicembre."*

[42] Ibid. Part 2, p. 44. *"Dico dunque, che il Bilancio del Libro non è altro, che un breve sommario, o sia Ristretto, o Compendio de i resti di tutti i conti scritti in esso, tanto a debito, quanto a credito, che nel tempo, che si vuol fare restano aperti, ridotto ad egualità."*

[43] Ibid. Part 2, p. 99. *"E se bene questo Bilancio si può fare in ogni tempo fra l'anno, e ogni volta, che ci verrà occasione, o ci parrà di farlo, si per vedere se nella scrittura del nostro Libro ci sia errore, come per vedere in che stato siano le cose nostre; Nondimeno il vero, proprio, e ordinario Bilancio è quello che si fa nel fine di ciascun'anno, quando si salda il libro. Dove è d'avvertire, che per Bilancio in questo luogo non intendiamo solamente quello col quale si va*

cercando la perfetta equalità nelle somme de i resti di tutti i conti debitori, e creditori del libro (perchè questo si può far subito senza veruna difficoltà, cavando indifferentemente i resti di tutti i conti, e paragonando fra di loro le somme di essi) ma quello, che si fa unitamente insieme col saldo de i conti del Libro . . . Poichè il Bilancio dice due cose, cioè la perfetta uguaglianza, dalla quale piglia il nome: e il saldo del Libro fatto in, tal modo, con tal ordine. Il quale (perchè per farlo bene s'ha da fare unitamente insieme col saldo di tutti i conti con la Spesa, e Entrata Generale, e con l'Esito) suol havere qualche difficoltà, e perciò richiede particolar sollecitudine, e attentione."

[44] Ibid. Part 2, p. 75. *"L'Esito poi dell' anno, o del Libro non è altro, che quel conto dove nel fine di ciascun' anno si tirano, e si riportano in breve i resti di tutti i Debitori, e Creditori particolari, secondo che rimangono nel Saldo del Libro."*

[45] Ibid. Part 2, p. 76. *"E si chiama con questo nome d'esito, perchè con questo conto si mostra la riuscita, e il successo dell'amministrazione di tutto l'anno. Poichè comparando questo conto dell'Esito con quello dell'Introito, si vede benissimo, in un occhiata dalla differenza loro, quanto, siano cresciuti, o scemati i debiti, o i crediti in quell'anno, e quanto sia migliorato, o deteriorato lo stato della Casa, o Collegio. Dove anco s'ha da notare la differenze, che è fra questo conto, e quello della Spesa, e Entrata Generale. Perchè questo ogn'anno s'estingue affatto, saldandolo con quel più, o con quel meno, che si sarà speso dell'Entrata havuta, riportando questa differenza alla Casa, o Collegio nostro: Ma quello dell'Esito resta non solo per mostrar la riuscita dell'anno presente, ma anco come per indice di tutto il capitale, che resta per il principio dell'anno seguente."*

[46] Peri, Giovanni Domenico. *Il negoziante* (Genova, 1638), part 1, p. 20.

[47] Ibid.

[48] Ibid.

[49] Bariola. Op. cit., part 2, p. 415.
Besta. Op. cit., vol. 3, p. 403.

[50] Bariola. Op. cit., part 2, p. 416.
Besta. Op. cit., vol. 3, p. 409.

[51] Bariola. Op. cit., part 2, p. 424.
Besta. Op. cit., vol. 3, p. 409.

[52] Bariola. Op. cit., part 2, p. 417.

[53] Ibid. Part 2, p. 425. *"e svolge anche il metodo a scrittura semplice, nel quale consiglia introdurre il Conto e (Avanzi e Disavanzi perchè con questo conto si salda tutte le altre partite altrimenti mai i saldi, si trovariano giusti.)"*

[54] Ibid. Part. 2, p. 417.
Besta. Op. cit., vol. 3, p. 413.

[55] Scali, Pietro Paolo. *Trattato del modo di tenere la scrittura* (Livorno, Fantechi, 1755), p. 7.

Chapter VII

THE THIRD CYCLE (1796 TO DATE)

THE French Revolution marked the beginning of a great political and social upheaval which transformed governments, finance, laws, and customs. Emancipated France was to serve as a model for the new social order, and she influenced Italy greatly. Napoleon's descent into Italy wrought many changes. He established the Cisalpine Republic with a democratic constitution modeled on that of the French Directorate. He terminated Venice's eleven hundred years' reign of independence and greatness, and dealt out the same fate to the other independent states. He abolished feudal laws and customs, introduced liberal constitutions, encouraged education, built roads, and carried on a vast program of reconstruction.

More important, however, to one interested in accounting, was his reorganization of the system of public finance. In the Kingdom of Italy, which succeeded the Cisalpine Republic, he had his minister, Prina, regularly publish the budget. The Kingdom's finances were shown to be seriously depleted and in chaotic condition. Prina introduced double entry in all government accounting, and under his capable management financial conditions were greatly improved.

Napoleon, with the establishment of the Empire, sought to organize its finances, and summoned to the task the most famous accountant in France, Count Mollien. Mollien established a system akin to double entry, which, however, did not prove satisfactory and was inferior to the system established in Italy by Prina. The historian Giuseppe Pecchio [1] quotes Napoleon as having praised the Italian accountants, in his private correspondence with Beauharnais, for their admirable administration of the treasury.

When Napoleon's regime ended with his defeat at Waterloo, Austria, eager to regain her authority in Italy, took possession of Lombardy and Venice and restored to their thrones all the despots of the Italian states overthrown by Napoleon. Napoleon's work was largely undone and absolute despotism triumphed again.

Austria used the cameral system of bookkeeping for the state finances. In the Middle Ages the *camera* (room) of the prince was the office in charge of the finances of the prince, and the method of bookkeeping used by these treasury officials became known as the cameral system. All transactions were considered as receipts and disbursements and were classified accordingly. This method is of the "family" type, because it is interested only in entries affecting the debtors and creditors of the state, and cash.[2] In 1761, Maria Theresa nominated a committee to study the installation of a method of accounting better suited to meet the requirements of government finance. After nine years (1770), the committee decided on double entry, but only two years later double entry was abandoned for the old cameral system. Wherever Austria ruled, the cameral system was used as the standard method of government bookkeeping. The system became imbedded in custom, and it was some time after the unification of Italy before the Italians, finally objecting to its cumbersomeness and other shortcomings, sought a more efficient system. Many new methods of state accounting were devised, among which the most important was that known as logismography.[3]

Thus Italy had to combat two foreign influences in accounting: the French influence and the Austrian. The former revolved about Dégranges's theory, applicable chiefly to mercantile accounting, and the latter centered upon the cameral system used in government accounting.

The nineteenth century, therefore, for our purposes divides itself into two periods: the first, lasting until the middle of the century, was one of resistance to foreign methods and theories of accounting; the second, instead, was a veritable battle of minds in which the theoretical basis of accounting was laid.[4]

THE EMERGENCE OF ACCOUNTING THEORY

Many new methods of bookkeeping were developed during the nineteenth century, but before discussing them, the fundamental theories of the account, or logismology, must be explained. These account theories are important, for they deal with the fundamentals of all bookkeeping. It may be safely stated that the sharp, animated polemics caused by opposing account theories were responsible to a large extent for placing the modern art of bookkeeping on a systematic basis.[5]

These theories are grouped into two major classes: the so-called personalistic-account theory and the positive or value-account theory. The first is based on the assumption that all accounts represent persons, whereas the second holds that accounts should be opened only to things.[6]

THE ANCIENT WRITERS

This process of personalizing accounts was used by the earliest writers, and may easily be traced to the genesis of the accounts themselves, which were first opened only to debtors and creditors. It was only natural that ancient writers, faced with the task of teaching laymen the nature of the account and the use of its conventional terms, should attribute to all accounts, even those not opened to debtors or creditors, the nature of a person, to be debited and credited as such, not as mere objects. The artifice was adopted primarily to facilitate explanation of the intricacies of the accounts, and it was cast off when its purpose was accomplished.[7] Paciolo used it frequently in the *Distinctio nona, Tractatus XI, De computis et scripturis* of his *Summa*. After correctly stating that the capital is the total resources of the proprietor and cash the total funds on hand, he went on to say that the proprietor assumes the position of creditor of his own capital.[8] In chapter 23, he explained that a branch of a store is in effect the debtor of the proprietor, so that the latter may debit the store for all he puts in it and credit it for all he takes out of it, just as he would do in the case of a debtor who contracted a debt and subsequently paid it.[9]

It is clear that here are the rudiments of the "personalistic" theory.[10]

Flori was even more explicit than his distinguished predecessor. He said that all inanimate accounts were to be thought of as real persons. For example, he explained, the cash account is like a person serving as a depositary to whom funds, entrusted and withdrawn, are debited and credited just as would be done in the case of a real person. Flori applied this to all other assets,[11] though it is obvious that he did not entertain for a moment the thought that all accounts were opened to real persons.[12] Similar quotations may be found in all early books on bookkeeping. The early writers used this fiction as an expedient for didactic purposes only; in those days it influenced bookkeeping procedure not at all, as is shown by the contemporary classifications of accounts.

The first known classification is that by Manzoni. He divided all accounts into two great groups, *conti vivi* (live accounts) and *conti morti* (dead accounts): the first, accounts opened to real persons, such as debtors and creditors, and the second, accounts opened to things, not persons.[13] Though Manzoni also used personalized accounts, nevertheless in his classification he severely segregated the accounts opened to persons from those opened to things. He would not allow the latter to be treated as persons.

Curiously enough, Manzoni's crude classification is found in many account theories of the nineteenth century. The only difference is in the change of names. The *conti vivi* become *conti personali* or *conti particolari*, and the *conti morti* become *conti impersonali, conti generali, conti sussidiari*, or *conti alle cose*.[14] It is about this classification and the process of personification that the controversies of the nineteenth century developed.

DEGRANGE AND THE CINQUECONTISTI SCHOOL

The first account theory to be developed was the French theory *des cinq comptes généraux* (of the five general accounts). Its adherents were known in Italy as the *cinquecontisti* (the five-accountists).

The French had received the mechanism of double entry from Italy and attempted to put it on a theoretical base. The resulting imperfect theory spread rapidly and its influence was felt especially in Italy, where it found strong supporters in Parmetler and Queirolo.

This theory generally is attributed to Edmond Dégrange, senior,[15] but before him Giraudeau in 1793 [16] had already written that *"les comptes généraux représentent le négociant lui même"* (the general accounts represent the proprietor himself). Dégrange, however, was more explicit. He divided accounts into two groups: the first embracing the accounts of debtors and creditors, and the second, the general accounts, which he considered as personal accounts of the proprietor. The second group included cash, merchandise, negotiable instruments receivable, negotiable instruments payable, and profit and loss; about them Dégrange writes: "To form an idea of these accounts one must know that they represent the proprietor for whom the books are kept, and that to debit one of these accounts is tantamount to debiting the proprietor himself under the name of a subsidiary account." [17] He asserts that all difficulties are removed by debiting the person who receives or the account of the object that is received, and by crediting the person who gives or the account of the object that is given.[18] This is the essence of the method.

The general accounts, which according to Giraudeau were to be at least seven and according to the elder Dégrange at least five, became in the writings of Dégrange, junior, rigidly fixed at five, with subdivisions for each of the five general accounts, as his father had already suggested. Dégrange junior offers for the first time the formula of the *cinquecontisti* school: *"débiter celui qui reçoit et créditer celui qui donne"* (debit him who receives and credit him who gives), which assumes all accounts to be strictly personal. When compared with the formula of Dégrange, senior, *". . . en débitant la personne . . . qui reçoit, ou le compt de l'objet que l'on reçoit; et en créditant . . . la personne qui fournit ou le compte de l'objet que l'on fournit,"* the personalistic character of the formula stands out in strong relief, for Dégrange, junior, omitted the alternative possibilities of impersonal or value accounts. This lack of flexibility was one cause for the ultimate rejection of the theory.

Dégrange's theory enjoyed a greater influence than it deserved. Imitators appeared everywhere, but their writings usually hurt the cause of the *cinquecontisti*, because they ignored the subdivision of the five general accounts of the two Dégranges and limited all the accounts, excepting debitors and creditors, to the unbelievable figure of five. Needless to say, such rigidity could not be maintained in practice.

The most noted followers of the Dégranges are Jaclot, Deplanque, Guibault, and Lefevre in France; Merten in Belgium; Parmetler (in his earlier writings) and Queirolo in Italy.[19]

FRANCESCO VILLA AND THE LOMBARD SCHOOL

On September 18, 1742, a society of accountants known as the Lombard School was founded at Milan. In the nineteenth century it was headed by Villa, and its chief purpose was to popularize a theory whose roots were deep in the practice of Italy's illustrious past, a theory which became a bulwark against the diffusion of the French theory.

Villa's system is not wholly personalistic, as was that of the *cinquecontisti*, but admitted both personal and impersonal accounts. The accounts were not fixed in number, but were infinite. They were classified as follows:

1. *Conti di deposito* (deposit accounts), including only impersonal accounts such as cash, merchandise, fixed assets.
2. *Conti personali* (personal accounts), including only accounts opened to individuals.
3. *Tre conti riassuntivi* (the three summary accounts), including the profit-and-loss and the initial and final balance accounts.

Manzoni's classification of *conti morti e vivi* (dead and live accounts) is discernible in the first two groups of Villa's classification.

Villa does not condemn Dégrange's theory outright, but belittles its importance. He says that the first four general accounts of the French theory (cash, merchandise, negotiable instruments receivable, and negotiable instruments payable) are nothing more than his *conti di deposito*, and the fifth general account, profit-and-loss, corresponds to his *conto riassuntivo* of profit and loss. [20]

The Lombard school checked the progress of the *cinquecontisti*, but it did not entirely discredit their theory; it remained for Francesco Marchi to do that.

HIPPOLYTE VANNIER

Vannier discusses accounting only as applied to mercantile enterprises. He classifies the accounts into three groups:

1. *Compte du commerçant* (proprietor's account), including the capital and profit-and-loss accounts;
2. *Comptes des valeurs commerçables* (commercial accounts), including all asset and liability accounts other than accounts receivable and payable;
3. *Comptes des correspondants*, the accounts of debtors and creditors.

In the second group, *comptes des valeurs commerçables*, are, among others, the following principal accounts: *marchandises* (merchandises), *caisse* (cash), *effets a reçevoir* (negotiable instruments receivable), *effets a payer* (negotiable instruments payable), *mobilier* (furniture and fixtures), *agencement* (branches), *frais de premier etablisement* (organization expenses), and *fonds de commerce* (commercial property). Vannier adds: "All these accounts must be regarded as

101

representing the employees of the firm. By 'marchandises,' must be understood the clerk in charge of receiving and issuing merchandise; by *caisse*, the cashier in charge of receipts and disbursements; by *effets a reçevoir*, the one who holds the portfolio of negotiable instruments; by *effets a payer*, the clerk responsible for entering in a special record the date of issuance and maturity of negotiable instruments payable; by *mobilier, agencement, frais de premier etablisements*, and *fonds de commerce*, the clerks who are responsible for these different accounts." [21]

It is evident that Vannier's theory is wholly personalistic, but it differs from Dégrange's theory in that Vannier does not consider all the accounts of his first two groups of the above classification as mere subdivisions of the proprietor's account. All of his accounts are personalized and are independent of the proprietor; he thereby avoids the paradox of the French theory, in which it appears that the proprietor debits and credits himself. [22]

FRANCESCO MARCHI

The first Italian personalistic theory of accounts is attributed to Francesco Marchi. In his famous book, *I Cinquecontisti*, published in 1867, he presented ideas, which, not knowing of Vannier's previous work, he thought to be new. He vigorously attacked Dégrange's theory and even disparaged it as "*l'inganne-vole teoria che viene insegnata negli instituti tecnici del Regno e fuori del Regno*" (the fraudulent theory that is taught in the technical institutes in the Kingdom and out of the Kingdom).

Marchi emphatically states that all accounts must be personal accounts opened to real persons because the proprietors are persons; cash, merchandise, and all other assets are placed in the hands of persons (employees), who are responsible to the proprietor for their custody, and of course debtors and creditors are persons. There is not one account, he finds, that is not chargeable to a real person. [23] He will have nothing to do with theories using impersonal accounts, and he severely condemns the *cinquecontisti* for considering the general accounts as a mere classification of the proprietor's account. He exposes the theory's fundamental fallacy by proving that the affairs of a business cannot be recorded in a system of bookkeeping by debiting and crediting the proprietor alone. Marchi's firm stand for realism is refreshing, and it is generally conceded that his work vindicated Italy's primacy in a field peculiarly Italian.

Marchi classified his accounts in four groups: [24]

1. The *consegnatari*, employees charged with handling the assets and liabilities of the enterprise;
2. The *corrispondenti*, debtors and creditors;
3. The *proprietario*, the proprietor;
4. The *gerente*, the person charged with the administration of the enterprise.

This classification bears out the complete personalistic aspect of Marchi's theory.

He foresees one objection which could be used against him and tries to meet it. In the majority of small enterprises, many assets and liabilities, which he places in the care of separate employees, are usually under the direct control of the proprietor, because obviously the enterprise is too small to afford a large staff. In such cases, he says, the proprietor assumes duties which ordinarily he would delegate to his subordinates, but he maintains that these duties are always to be thought of as separate and distinct from those which are his properly, and they are to be treated on the books accordingly.[25]

The personalistic properties of Marchi's theory are brought out again strongly in his general formula for entering transactions into his accounts: "Debit him who receives a value or who becomes debtor for value, and credit him who gives a value or becomes creditor for value."[26]

Marchi's caustic treatment of Dégrange's theory sounded its death knell. The theory was discredited and no longer taught in the schools, while in practice it was discarded for Marchi's more rational system. Even Parmetler, a strong supporter of the cinquecontisti, publicly repudiated the French theory and became an enthusiastic follower of Marchi, despite the latter's derisive criticism of his work.[27]

GIUSEPPE CERBONI

Cerboni, accepting Marchi's personalistic theory, says that "only real and living accounts, referring to real persons, with real debits and credits, can exist; there can be no dead accounts, accommodation accounts, artificial accounts which deal in abstractions, whether administrative, economic, or bookkeeping."[28]

Cerboni had to decide which were the real persons for whom such accounts were to be opened. Here again he follows Marchi and considers an enterprise as composed of the proprietario (proprietor), amministratore (administrator or executive), agenti consegnatari (employees or, as he calls them, consignees or depositaries), and the corrispondenti (debtors and creditors).

Like Marchi, he again states that, when a proprietor manages his own business, he assumes the double characteristic of proprietor and administrator and that the same doubling up of personalities occurs when the administrator undertakes duties usually delegated to employees.[29] But then, leaving Marchi, he concludes that the proprietor, whether or not he manages his enterprise, is the creditor of its assets and the debtor of its liabilities, and vice-versa for the consegnatori and corrispondenti.[30]

To understand this conclusion, it must be realized that Cerboni believed all enterprises, whether in the field of business or government, to be fundamentally divided into two sections opposed to each other: on one side the proprietor alone, and on the other side the *amministratori, consegnatari,* and *corrispondenti.*[31] Rossi says that these two sections are like two opposing personalities, two entities with eternally antagonistic interests. They were respectively named the *proprietario* and the *azienda* (the latter's nearest equivalent in English is "business entity," meaning a unit complete in itself, and independent of the proprietor.)

Cerboni, pursuing this argument further, says that a credit of the proprietor corresponds to a debit of the *agenti* and *corrispondenti,* and the reverse. The function of the *amministratore* is to keep a debit and a credit balance between the proprietor on the one hand and the *agenti* and *corrispondenti* on the other[32]

On these premises, Cerboni offers the following practical rule: "Every set of books must begin with the opening of two accounts, one for the *proprietario* and the other for the *azienda* (i.e. *agenti* and *corrispondenti*), and these accounts must always balance with each other, so that the credit of the *proprietario* is constantly equal to the debit of the *agenti* and *corrispondenti,* and the debit of the former will always equal the credit of the latter." [33] The first of these two accounts is called by Cerboni *conto del proprietario, conto principale,* or *conto del mandante;* the second one is termed *conto dell'azienda, conto agenziale,* or *conto degli agenti e dei corrispondenti.* These two accounts are the pivot of Cerboni's system and together they constitute the so-called balance of logismography (*bilancia logismografica*).

Cerboni advanced a new concept of rights and duties, which he built upon the interrelations of the opposing interests of the proprietor and the *azienda.* He says the proprietor has the right to command and the *azienda* the duty to carry out his orders regarding the administration of the enterprise. On the other hand, the *azienda* has the right to acknowledgment of the fulfillment of such orders, and this is the duty of the proprietor. Cerboni then dogmatically states that the term "right" is equivalent to the term "credit" and "duty" to "debit," and since in double entry debits and credits are equal, he concludes that duties equal rights. To support this, he contends that a right of a person never arises without the imposition of a corresponding duty upon another person.

Never at any time does Cerboni make his argument about rights and duties convincing, and its obvious weakness made it vulnerable to the attacks of his opponents. Nevertheless, Cerboni thought that, by the opposition of these rights and duties between the proprietor on one side and the *agenti* and *corrispondenti* on the other, he had finally surmounted the major accounting difficulty of his time. He had discovered, he believed, the reason for debiting and crediting accounts in double entry. He resolved the whole system of debits and credits into a system of moral duties and rights.

Marchi, in developing his personalistic theory, had in mind only the justification of the actual practices of the profession of accounting. Cerboni, instead, used his theory to create the totally new system of logismography. It caused radical changes in government and private bookkeeping and for many years held undisputed sway over all theories of accounting.

The most prominent of his followers are Giovanni Rossi, Michele Riva, Clitofonte Bellini, Francesco Bonalumi, and Sanguinetti Achille.[34]

FABIO BESTA

The personalistic account theory was attacked and dislodged from its place of eminence by the appearance of a theory with fundamentals irreconcilably opposed to its own. This is the famous *teorica dei conti ai valori* (value theory of accounts), also called *Teorica positiva del conto* (positive theory of the account), developed by Professor Fabio Besta, known throughout Italy as the *maestro di ragioneria* (master of accountancy).

Besta arrived at his theory by way of a profound and painstaking historical research. Delving into ancient bookkeeping manuscripts, he established the fact that the first accounts used in bookkeeping were those opened to real debtors and creditors, in which the terms *dare* (debit) and *avere* (credit) meant respectively "to give" and "to have." He observed, however, that as bookkeeping gradually came to include all the elements of proprietorship, the terms *dare* and *avere* met the altered conditions by imperceptible changes in meaning. *Dare* became associated with debit mutations and *avere* with credit mutations of all assets and liabilities. He furthermore found that nominal accounts (i.e. expense and income accounts) originated in the conduct of business for third persons, where transactions were consummated by agents for their absent principals. In such cases, *dare* necessarily meant a confirmation of credit mutations and *avere* a confirmation of debit mutations of assets or liabilities.

Upon these findings, Besta erected his account theory. He established the meaning which the continuous evolution of accounting practice had attached to the terms *dare* and *avere*, and he condemned the imputation of arbitrary meanings to these terms, as many of his predecessors had done.

Besta's account theory is simple. He begins by stating that bookkeeping is "the medium for prompt rendering of information regarding cash, accounts receivable, fixed assets, interest on investments, . . . etc., and it is evident to everyone that rapid and certain accessibility of such information is impossible without recording in the same place the mutations occurring in each of these objects. This accepted, each group of entries referring to an object constitutes an account." [35]. He defines the account as "a series of entries regarding a clearly defined object, commensurable and mutable, with the function of recording information about the condition and amount of the object at a particular moment and of the changes it undergoes, so that the information may be

105

available at any time."[36] Beśta's two fundamental tenets are already evident:

1. The accounts are opened directly to the elements of capital (capital, a complex of elements which together constitute an object of bookkeeping).
2. The accounts are intended primarily to put in evidence the values of these elements and their mutations.

These principles are obviously opposed to a personalistic treatment of accounts. The accounts are opened directly to objects, not to any intervening person, and they indicate money values, not fictitious moral values of rights and duties as in certain other systems. In undermining the personalistic theory, Beśta dealt a fatal blow to Cerboni's system of logismography and to a number of other systems founded on the same theory.

One of Beśta's great merits is that he followed reality faithfully, gathering his proofs from his severe application of the historical method. His interpretation of accounting justly became the basis of modern practice. Rossie tried against Beśta the same withering attack that Marchi had so successfully employed against the *cinquecontisti*, but, unlike the latter, Beśta's theory was firmly based on sound principles and easily withstood all onslaughts.

Among the most eminent of Beśta's followers are Giuseppe Siboni, Vittorio Alfieri, Carlo Ghidiglia, Pietro D'Alvise, Benedetto Lorusso, Vincenzo Vianello, Francesco De Gobbis, Francesco Scardini, Antonio Sella, and Francesco Saporetti.[37] Beśta died in 1922.

THEORIES OF DOUBLE ENTRY

All methods of bookkeeping may be said to have a series of norms, or standards, governing procedure, and a series of principles underlying these norms. The essential characteristics of double entry, throughout its long evolutionary process, have remained fairly constant, and its standards, as set forth by the numerous authors of the last four centuries, have changed little. On the other hand, the principles in terms of which authors have been wont to rationalize the system of double entry have varied widely. By these principles, students have sought to explain the nature of the accounts and to determine what should be their form and number, the procedure for debiting and crediting each account, and finally the relationship between one entry and another and between one account and another.

Beśta groups together the nature of accounts, the number of accounts, and the determination of their common measure of value as essential parts of the general account theory, as distinguished from the special theory of any given method of double entry.[38]

RUDIMENTARY THEORIES

Before the nineteenth century, authors were generally content to state, rather than to prove, the constant equality of debits and credits, as if the phenomenon were natural and self-evident.

The author of the work gathered by Paciolo into his *Summa*, after having asserted that in every journal entry the debit and credit must be indicated, added that "for every entry in the journal, two entries must be made in the ledger, that is, one as a debit and the other as a credit." He said further that "the debit entry must bear the page number of the credit, and vice-versa. . . . It is thus that all entries of the ledger are linked together. No entry must be entered in debit which is not also entered in credit, and the reverse; this determines the balance of the ledger, as it is set forth in the balance account."[39]

Manzoni added little to this. He observed that the merchant must ascertain the debtor and the creditor involved in each transaction, and described this as the most difficult phase of the art of bookkeeping.[40]

Subsequent writers, even as late as the nineteenth century, could contribute little more to an understanding of the principles of double entry.

THEORIES BASED ON INDUCTIVE LOGIC

Some authors, using the inductive method, tried to prove the equality of debits and credits by contrasting the shortcomings of single entry with the virtues of double entry.

De La Porte, one of the first French theorists, discussed single entry at length, calling it *méthode imparfait* (imperfect method), and then spoke of the Italian manner "*de tenir les livres a parties doubles*" (of using the double-entry system), which he proclaimed as the *méthode parfait* (perfect method); he added "that all merchants with large businesses use double-entry books, because they contain the whole of their affairs." [41]

Similarly, Francesco Villa said: "The principal object of double entry is to overcome the imperfections of single entry." [42] Accordingly, he suggested that, to the deposit and personal accounts of single entry, there be added the three summary accounts of his system of double entry.

Villa submitted no proofs that his three summary accounts are essential to a system of double entry; he could not have produced them. His three accounts include the opening and closing balance accounts and the profit-and-loss account. These three accounts are not essential to double entry; there are several means of opening and closing books other than through balance accounts, and there are several ways of summarizing nominal accounts. Villa's three summary accounts cannot serve as a base of a theory.[43] They are a purely arbitrary classification, contributing nothing of lasting value.

THEORIES BASED ON THE INTERRELATION OF ACCOUNTS

Many tried to demonstrate the debit and credit balance by showing the interplay between asset and liability accounts and nominal accounts.

Crippa, a prominent author and contemporary of Villa, said that all transactions may be completely classified and recorded by use of the asset and liability and the nominal accounts. He observed that transactions affecting only asset and liability accounts, excluding withdrawals from and additions to capital, give rise to the double effect of debit and credit, but produce no corresponding change in proprietorship, while entries involving both asset and liability and nominal accounts do affect proprietorship and the nominal accounts show the resulting increase or decrease. He cited this interaction between asset and liability and nominal accounts as a proof of the equality of debits and credits.[44]

Similar notions are found in the work of the German writers Kurzbauer, Löw, and Stern, and the French writer, J. B. De Launay.

Vincenzo Gitti began by stating the proprietorship equation, using A for assets, P for liabilities and N for original net worth:

$$A - P = N; \text{ or } A = P + N$$

Gitti, like Crippa, correctly observed that transactions involving only asset and liability accounts do not cause a change in net worth:

$$A' - P' = N; \text{ or } A' = P' + N$$

But when nominal accounts are involved, net worth does change, and he used the additional symbols R for increase and S for decrease of net worth:

$$A' - P' = N + R - S; \text{ or } A' + S = P' + N + R$$

He then stated that double entry has nominal accounts for R and S and thus constantly maintains the equilibrium between the asset and liability and the nominal elements of capital, believing he has thus proved the debit and credit equality of accounts.

Besta says the point of departure of these men is correct, but their proof of the equality of debits and credits is erroneous. None of them gave recognition to the values of the accounts, though it is an equality of value, alone, which occurs.[45]

PERSONALISTIC THEORIES

Followers of personalistic-account theories developed another rationalization of double entry. Their argument generally ran as follows: All accounts are opened to persons and the accounts show real debits and credits; a debit cannot arise without a corresponding credit, and vice-versa; therefore, a sum cannot be entered in debit which is not also entered in credit, and vice-versa. This is the syllogism used by those who base their theories of double entry on the concept of personalistic accounts. Besta's confutation of the personalistic theory invalidates this premise and thus also invalidates all double-entry theories based on the personalistic-account theory.

Among the authors of this school is Dégrange. He based his theory on the concept that the five general accounts are opened to the proprietor, and that only by debiting and crediting these general accounts is the totality of the merchant's affairs embraced and the balance of the books maintained. To give weight to his argument, he quoted his famous formula: "Debit the person who receives or the account of the object received, and credit the person who gives or the account of the object given." [46]

His son started out by saying that in double entry every entry "*doit comprendre toujours un debiteur et un crediteur*," that is, implies the existence of a debtor and a creditor, thus dogmatically stating, without demonstration, a principle requiring proof. He thereafter followed in his father's footsteps.

Francesco Marchi fiercely attacked the French theory and all other theories which were based on what he considered erroneous concepts of the account. He wanted accounts opened only to real persons, not to things or fictitious persons, as advocated by Villa and Dégrange. He wanted accounts opened to the *proprietario* (proprietor), *consegnatari* (employees, depositaries), and *corrispondenti* (debtors and creditors).

He thought he had proved the principle of equality of debits and credits when he said that an entry must be registered twice, once in debit and the other in credit — thus his fundamental rule: "Debit him who receives a value or who becomes debtor for value, and credit him who gives a value or becomes creditor for value. [47]

He condemned the use of fictions, but was not above employing the fiction of ascribing more personalities than one to the proprietor if he assumed duties usually delegated to his subordinates, maintaining separate accounts for each of these several personalities.

Marchi's demonstration of the equality of debits and credits, as in the case of the authors he attacks, was not conclusive; his system also was based on the erroneous personalistic-account theory. [48]

THE VALUE THEORY

Fabio Besta, [49] starting from the principle that all accounts are opened directly to the objects, developed a sound theory of double entry and demonstrated the equality of debits and credits. He turned his attention to the values of the accounts and demonstrated by mathematical methods that the debit values constantly equal the credit values. He expressed the original capital in an equation

JOURNAL — GRAND — LIVRE[1]

Vendém au XI (date)	Journal commencé le 1ª Vendemaire au XI	Total des affaires au journal (journal column)	Marchandise générales (merchandise in general)		Caisse (cash)		Billets à recevoir (negotiable instruments receivable)		Billets à payer (negotiable instruments payable)		Profits et pertes (profits and losses)		Divers comptes (miscellaneous accounts)		Total de chaque compte particulier au grand-livre (total of each general ledger acct)	
			Débit	Crédit	Débit	Crédit	Débit	Crédit	Débit	Crédit	Débit	Crédit	Débit	Crédit	Débit	Crédit
		Francs	Francs	Francs												
	1 Marchandises générales a Pierre pour 10 tonneau de vin rouge achetès à Pierre, à 300 francs le tonneau $\frac{1}{6.1}$	3,000—	3,000											3,000		
	etc.	etc.											etc.		etc.	etc.
	27 Total des affaires faſtes en vendemiaire	166,616	55,960	48,056	63,674	16,162	26,000	12,000	11,000	24,960	2,081	20,938	7,900	14,500	166,616	166,616

Total des affaires au grand-livre

Débit	Crédit
55,960	48,056
63,674	46,162
26,000	12,000
11,000	24,960
2,081	20,938
7,900	14,500
166,616	166,616

110

which is modified with the occurrence of transactions affecting assets, liabilities, expenses, income, and capital; the equation in the end still holds true, proving his hypothesis. Besta split his proof into a series of fundamental theorems, taking up separate variations successively.

Besta's theory is self-consistent and is in complete harmony with the practices of the profession.[50]

METHODS OF DOUBLE ENTRY

Study of the theories of accounts and of double entry facilitates an understanding of the various methods of bookkeeping evolved during the nineteenth century.

THE METHODS OF DÉGRANGE

The French system, it will be remembered, divided the accounts into two major groups: the debtor and the creditor accounts and the proprietor's five general accounts, which were cash, merchandise, negotiable instruments receivable, negotiable instruments payable, and profit-and-loss. Each of these general accounts had subdivisions, which gave the French method the flexibility needed to meet the requirements of different types of business.

The fundamental weakness of this system was that the five general accounts and their subdivisions were opened to the proprietor personally. Though this was the creed of the *cinquecontisti*, nevertheless their practical sense forbade them to apply the principle literally, and under the fiction of proprietor's accounts they opened accounts to all the elements of proprietorship.

This practical sense was evident again in Dégrange's *journal-grand-livre* (*giornale-mastro*, literally journal-ledger). This book combined the ledger and the journal in one record; it had one journal column, and debit and credit columns for his five general accounts, plus a column for miscellaneous accounts. An example taken from Dégrange's *Supplément à la tenue des livres rendu facile* is given on page 110. Besta found the principal defect of this record was the crowding of accounts into the space of one page. Use of insert sheets might diminish the importance of this criticism, but it would still apply in the case of firms requiring a large number of accounts, for the book would then be cumbersome even though insert sheets were used.

The columnar-book system is generally considered to be a form of record peculiarly American, but this belief is unfounded. Dégrange was its inventor. He made use of the system long before he published it in 1804, after Edward Thomas Jones had secured a patent in England on a system closely resembling his own.[51] Many copied and developed this form of record, and its origin was ignored or forgotten. It became known as the American method as early as 1852.[52]

THE METHODS OF VILLA AND MARCHI

Neither Villa nor Marchi attempted to make innovations, but both developed theories in justification of existing practices. Their chief purpose was the overthrow of the *cinquecontisti*.

Marchi's theory, however, differed from Villa's in that Villa opened accounts to things as well as to persons, while Marchi insisted that only accounts opened to real persons were true and that impersonal accounts were fictitious.

These differences did not prevent both men from advocating very similar methods of bookkeeping. Each derived his inspiration from the Italian orthodox tradition of double entry. Their methods, of course, are more synthetic and refined in form, but are not in conflict with the system of the ancients. They need not be studied in detail, because they do not embody changes requiring explanation.

LOGISMOGRAPHY

On the eighteenth of February, 1862, the first Italian Parliament was opened. The new kingdom was unified politically, but administratively and fiscally it was still a medley of small states. Italy had to be welded economically with one national budget if she was to survive in her struggle for existence. This was no easy task. The small states — incorporated into the young nation — did not possess uniform fiscal and bookkeeping systems that could be easily fused together. Because of the Austrian influence, the systems in use were mostly of the cameral type; not one of them was double entry. They were a heterogeneous mass of single-entry systems.

The need of Parliament was to find a suitable bookkeeping system to apply throughout the kingdom. Not much was accomplished toward this end until Cambray-Digny, financier of distinction and able accountant, became prime minister. On February 4, 1868, he submitted to Parliament a plan for reducing all government bookkeeping to a double-entry basis. Heated discussion raged over this proposal, but it became law on April 22, 1869, to be put into effect during the following year.

Then, Professor Michele Riva's book appeared.[53] Riva was the accountant of the municipality of Ferrara and set for himself the task of proving the inapplicability of double entry to all phases of government finances. He pointed out the differences between a private enterprise and a public enterprise. Government, he said, had two functions: the legislative, concerned with creating the budget and determining the sources of revenue, and the executive, concerned with collection of revenue and authorizing the disbursements voted in the budget. The State, he held, needed two types of bookkeeping: one for purposes of the budget and all the rights and duties it gives rise to, and the other for control of receipts and disbursements. Double entry would apply only to the latter, which deals with economic facts, and not to the former, which deals with estimates and moral values.

Riva's book influenced official opinion, and the law of 1869 was prevented from going into effect. Thus, instead of a double-entry system incorporating the three elements of government finance (budget, rights and duties entailed by the budget, and receipts and disbursements), government bookkeeping still remained an unrelated mass of reports of receipts and disbursements.[54]

This was the state of affairs when Giuseppe Cerboni published his first work on logismography in 1872,[55] setting forth his new theory and its famous six axioms and corollaries.[56] This book caused a sensation. The system he advocated was immediately applied by the omnibus company of Florence and by the administrative department of the war ministry, of which Cerboni was administrative director.

As a result of his new system, which seemed to resolve the difficulties of government bookkeeping, Cerboni was made accountant general of the state in 1876. This gave him the opportunity to apply his logismography on a more ambitious scale. He extended it to include all state accounting, and thus for the first time the three elements of government administration were dovetailed into a single system of bookkeeping.

Fundamentally, logismography is based on the personalizing of all accounts, which enabled Cerboni to introduce into accounting the concept of morality.

Only two fundamental accounts with their subdivisions are needed in logismography: the proprietor's account and the account which groups together debtors, creditors, and employees, that is, all persons with whom the proprietor has to do. Cerboni assumed that the interests of these two groups were irreconcilably opposed to each other, and upon their interrelations built up a precarious structure of moral values. In applying logismography to government bookkeeping, Cerboni changed the names of his two fundamental accounts from *proprietario* (proprietor) and *agenti e corrispondenti* (employees and debtors and creditors) to *stato* (the state, i.e., Parliament with its legislative prerogatives) and *governo* (the government, i.e., the executive who executes the laws of Parliament).

Cerboni says that the State has the right to determine the budget and the government has the duty to accept it and carry it out. But when the budget is executed, the government has the right to have this fact acknowledged and the State has the duty to recognize it. Translated into bookkeeping terms, this means that, when the budget is approved by Parliament, the State is credited and the government is debited for the sums appropriated in the budget, and that, when sums necessary to meet the budget are raised through taxation and disbursed

Numéro des parties	INDICATION DES OPÉRATIONS ADMINISTRATIVES	MONTANT des ARTICLES en partie double	EXERCICE PATRIMONIAL 1880			
			BALANCE ENTRE L'ETAT ET SES AGENTS ET CORRESPONDA			
			L'Etat pour la gestion générale patrimoniale, économique (Comptes spécifiques et statistiques) **A, A**^{bis}		Les Agents et les Corres. pour la gestion générale écon. (Comptes juridique **B**	
			Doit	Avoir	Doit	A
1	2	3	4	5	6	
	Report . . .	36,944,906,261 63	8,828,838,317 95	1,501,478,023 53	1,501,478,023 53	8,828,8
30	**Clôture des comptes et résultats généraux** . . . . (a)	10,832,870,860 06	. . . .	. . . .	. . . .	
	Exercice du budget.					
	RECETTES. Recettes prévues . . . . L. 1,412,791,084 75 Id. constatées . . . . 1,439,368,496 87 Id. constatées en plus	26,577,412 12	. . . .	. . . .	. . .	
	Balance aritméthique du budget des recettes		. . . .	. . . .	. . .	
	DÉPENSES. Dépenses prévues . . . . . . L. 1,401,631,403 68 Id. constatées . . . . 1,420,226,726 38 Id. constatées en plus	18,595,322 70	. . . .	. . . .	. . .	
	Balance aritméthique du budget des dépenses. . . .		. . . .	. . . .	. . .	
	CONTRÔLE. Recettes prévues . . . . . . L. 1,412,791,084 75 Dépenses prévues . . . . 1,401,631,403 68 Excédant présumé	11,159,681 07	. . . .	. . . .	. . .	
	Recettes constatées . . . . L. 1,439,368,496 87 Dépenses constatées . . . . 1,420,226,726 38 Excédant réel de l'exercice . . .	19,141,770 49	. . . .	. . . .	. . .	
	Recettes constatées en plus . L. 26,577,412 12 Dépenses constatées en plus . . . . 18,595,322 70 Différence entre le total des recettes et des dépenses . . .	7,982,089 42	. . . .	. . . .	. . .	
	§ II — Exercice patrimonial.					
	Excédant du passif sur l'actif au 1er janvier 1880 . . . . −7,390,171,609 80	−7,390,171,609 80				
	Frais et diminutions dans l'actif de l'inventaire général . −1,438,666,708 15	−1,438,666,708 15				
	Total du passif	−8,828,838,317 95	. . . .	8,828,838,317 95	. . . .	8,828
	Revenus et diminutions dans le passif de l'inventaire général . . . +1,501,478,023 53		. . .	. . . .	1,501,478,023 53	1,501,478,023 53
	Augmentation du patrimoine . . . . + 62,811,315 38	+ 62,811,315 38				
	Excédant passif au 31 décembre 1880	−7,327,360,294 42	7,327,360,294 42	. . . .	7,327,360,294 42	7,327,360,294 42
	Balance aritméthique des écritures de l'Etat	55,188,593,691 91	8,828,838,317 95	8,828,838,317 95	8,828,838,317 95	8,828

(a) Le total de L. 10,832,870,860. 06 inscrit dans les 3ème et 16ème colonnes représente la somme obtenue en additionnant les permutations de cette partie n° 30 dans la colonne 4ème

EXERCICE DU BUDGET 1880								PERMUTATIONS ET COMPENSATIONS	
BALANCE ENTRE L'ETAT ET LES ORDONNATEURS DES RECETTES				BALANCE ENTRE L'ETAT ET LES ORDONNATEURS DES DÉPENSES					
L'Etat pour les recettes prévues et pour celles constatées (Comptes législatifs) C		Les Ordonnateurs des recettes pour les recettes prévues et pour celles constatées (Comptes administratifs) D		L'Etat pour les dépenses prévues et pour celles constatées (Comptes législatifs) E		Les Ordonnateurs des dépenses pour les dépenses prévues et pour celles constatées (Comptes administratifs) F		TOTAUX	INDICATION DES DÉVELOPPEMENTS
Doit 8	Avoir 9	Doit 10	Avoir 11	Doit 12	Avoir 13	Doit 14	Avoir 15	16	17
368,496 87	1,412,791,084 75	1,412,791,084 75	1,439,368,496 87	1,401,631,403 68	1,420,226,726 38	1,420,226,726 38	1,401,631,403 68	20,940,572,208 47	
.....	.....	.....	.....	.....	.....	.....	.....	10,832,970,860 06	A. A-1. Abis, B. C. D. E. F.
.....	26,577,412 12	26,577,412 12	.....						
368,496 87	1,439,368,496 87	1,439,368,496 87	1,439,368,496 87						
.....	.....	.....	.....	18,595,322 70	.....	.....	18,595,322 70		
.....	.....	.....	.....	1,420,226,726 38	1,420,226,726 38	1,420,226,726 38	1,420,226,726 38		
.....	.....	.....	.....	11,159,681 07	.....	.....	11,159,681 07		
.....	.....	.....	.....	.....	19,141,770 49	19,141,770 49	.....		
.....	.....	.....	.....	7,982,089 42	.....	.....	7,982,089 42		
368,496 87	1,439,368,496 87	1,439,368,496 87	1,439,368,496 87	1,439,368,496 87	1,439,368,496 87	1,439,368,496 87	1,439,368,496 87	31,773,443,068 53	

éveloppements A. A-1, A bis, B, C, D, E, F.

according to the budget, the State is debited and the government credited, thus canceling the first entry and liquidating the budget. This is the gist of logismography, and it indicates the reason why only two fundamental accounts are necessary.

Cerboni went to great pains to show that in logismography debits and credits are equal, just as in double entry; but he went further than double entry: he made the two fundamental accounts equal to each other in every respect. The debits of one equal the credits of the other, and the credits of the first equal the debits of the latter; logismography is a system of quadruple entry. All transactions are passed through the proprietor's account, so that the latter will show immediately any changes occurring in net worth. For example, upon the receipt of cash the cashier is debited and the proprietor credited, and then the debtor is credited and the proprietor debited.

This is the backbone of Cerboni's system, but there is more to it. Stated as it is here, it would involve just double the amount of work that is needed in double entry, because of its quadruple-entry characteristic. Cerboni, however, claimed for this system the advantage of brevity, synthesis, and ready availability of data necessary for the conduct of business. These are all attributes which descriptive, analytic double entry lacked up to the time Cerboni wrote.

How did Cerboni coördinate his system of logismography? First of all he eliminated the ledger proper, as it is known in double entry, and in its place he substituted an enlarged journal,[57] which carried, besides the journal entries, the two fundamental accounts. These two accounts, of course, could be and in practice were split up into as many accounts as were necessary for the proper exposition of the affairs of government or business, subject to the limitation of the number of columns that could be placed on a double page of the book, insert sheets being unknown at the time. Brevity was achieved by omitting explanations, a fundamental characteristic of double entry.

Cerboni was chiefly interested in knowing the changes occurring in capital. To this end, he classified all transactions into two groups. In the first, he placed the transactions which either increased or diminished capital, and named them *modificazioni* (i.e., modifications or changes). In double entry, such transactions are entered in nominal accounts. In the second group, he placed all transactions which neither increased nor diminished capital, including the exchange of one asset for another or one liability for another, the elimination of a liability by surrender of an asset, or the acquisition of an asset by an increase of liabilities; these he called *permutazioni* (permutations).

In the fundamental journal accounts, Cerboni entered only transactions which "modify" capital. All other transactions were entered in the journal column proper and carried out to the last column entitled *permutazioni*, the purpose of which was to relieve the fundamental accounts of transactions not modifying capital. The device served also to unify the system, though clarity and valuable information were sacrificed for the necessary brevity. Cerboni retained the correct net balances of these fundamental accounts, but he gave up entirely the information supplied by the aggregate of total debits and credits of each account and account group. Double entry provides valuable ratios from comparisons between groups of accounts, current assets and current liabilities, for example. Such information is not available in logismography.

The *permutazioni* column served as a posting medium for permutation entries to subsidiary schedules, which Cerboni named *svolgimenti*. The *svolgimenti* had as many columns as were necessary for the allocation of permutation entries. The schedules had titles and were distinguished, for cross-index purposes, by capital letters. The entries in the journal were numbered consecutively to facilitate tracing them from the schedules. The permutation column also had a column where the capital letters of the schedules were entered.

These *svolgimenti* stood in the same relation to the journal as subsidiary ledgers in double entry stand to the main ledger. This is evident when it is considered that the ledger is the foundation of double entry, whereas the fundamental accounts in the journal provide the basis of logismography.

On pages 114 and 118 are shown examples of the journal and *svolgimenti*. They are taken from Cerboni's *Memoire sur l'importance d'unifier les études de la comptabilité*, and are typical examples of government bookkeeping as conceived in logismography. The journal shows the tie between the journal proper, the proprietorship accounts, and the budget, with the permutation column at the end. The example on page 118 shows a summary of entries, some of which are described as follows: Entry number 1 is a deficit of approximately seven billion lire carried over from the previous year and entered in the balance-sheet section as a debit to the state and a credit to its agents, debtors, and creditors. Entries 2 and 3, in the budget section, show the estimated receipts and disbursements. For receipts, the state is credited and government officials debited; for disbursements, the procedure is reversed. Entry number 6 shows the actual receipts entered both in the balance-sheet section and in the receipts section of the budget. In the former, the state is credited and its agents debited; in the latter, the state is debited and government officials credited, this last entry canceling a portion of the estimated receipts set up in entry number 2. The amount in the permutation column does not represent true receipts, but rather reimbursements. Entry number 11 represents actual disbursements. Again, both the balance-sheet section and the disbursement section of the budget are affected. The entries are the reverse of those recording actual receipts. The amount in the permutation column stands for payments of assets purchased, which therefore is not a decrease of net worth,

Numéro des parties	INDICATIONS	COLONNES équivalentes à la 4me e 5me du journal Doit 2	COLONNES équivalentes à la 4me e 5me du journal Avoir 3	COLONNE équivalente à partie de la 16me du journal 4	CRÉDITS Recettes recouvrées Doit 5	CRÉDITS Recettes constatées Avoir 6	DÉBITS Sommes disposées Doit 7	DÉBITS Sommes payées Avoir 8	CRÉDITS Recettes recouvrées Doit 9	CRÉDITS Recettes constatées Avoir 10	DÉBITS Sommes disposées Doit 11	DÉBITS Sommes payées Avoir
1	Actif et passif de l'exercice précédent	7,990.171,609 80	....	211,519,941 10	....	....	....	....	....	....	....	.
6	Constatation des recettes *effectives*	....	1,214,913,818 85	23,700,420 41	....	1,238,614,239 26	....	....	....	....	....	.
7	Constatation des recettes pour *Mouvement des capitaux*	....	....	41,940,417 23	....	....	....	....	....	41,940,417 23	....	.
8	Constatation des recettes pour *Construction des chemins de fer*	....	....	67,755,713 30	....	....	....	....	....	....	....	.
9	Constatation des recettes pour *Parties d'ordre*	....	....	90,883,109 32	....	....	....	....	....	....	....	.
10	Différence dans la constatation des recettes pour *Parties d'ordre*	....	175,017 76	....	....	....	....	....	....	....	....	.
11	Constatation des dépenses *effectives*	1,115,063,818 25	....	81,614,353 64	....	....	1,196,678,171 89	....	....	....	....	.
12	Constatation des dépenses pour *Mouvement des capitaux*	....	....	64,678,286 29	....	....	....	....	....	....	64,678,286 29	.
13	Constatation des dépenses pour *Construction des chemins de fer*	....	....	67,987,158 88	....	....	....	....	....	....	....	.
14	Constatation des dépenses pour *Parties d'ordre*	....	....	90,883,109 32	....	....	....	....	....	....	....	.
15	Variations aux résidus actifs des budgets des années précédentes	12,231,415 83	....	....	....	....	....	....	....	....	....	.
16	Variations aux résidus passifs des budgets des années précédentes	....	10,308,413 56	....	....	....	....	....	....	....	....	.
17	Perception des recettes de 1880	....	....	1,297,368,043 72	1,169,808,552 43	....	....	....	34,262,251 18	....	....	.
18	Perception des résidus actifs	....	....	78,191,607 74	....	....	....	....	....	....	....	.
20	Paiements effectues en compte de compétence	....	....	1,211,356,330 57	....	....	....	1,053,182,841 90	....	....	....	58,605.
21	Paiements effectués en compte des résidus passifs	....	....	173,257,370 04	....	....	....	....	....	....	....	.
22	Augmentations survenues dans l'actif patrimonial de l'Etat	....	247,295,547 62	....	....	....	....	....	....	....	....	.
23	Diminutions survenues dans l'actif patrimonial de l'Etat	257,961,519 33	....	....	....	....	....	....	....	....	....	.
24	Augmentations survenues dans le passif de l'Etat	43,896,368 55	....	....	....	....	....	....	....	....	....	.
25	Diminutions survenues dans le passif de l'Etat	....	23,785,225 74	....	....	....	....	....	....	....	....	.
28	Emission de décrets de décharge en faveur des comptables débiteurs	111,586 19	....	....	....	....	....	....	....	....	....	.
		8,828,838,317 95	1,501,478,023 53	3,501,135,861 56	1,169,808,552 43	1,238,614,239 26	1,196,678,171 89	1,053,182,841 90	34,262,251 18	41,940,417 23	64,678,286 29	58,695.
30	Clôture des comptes	....	7,327,360,294 42	263,097,370 68	68,805,686 83	....	....	143,495,329 99	7,678,166 05	....	....	5,962.
		8,828,838,317 95	8,828,838,317 95	3,764,233,232 24	1,238,614,239 26	1,238,614,239 26	1,196,678,171 89	1,196,678,171 89	41,940,417 23	41,940,417 23	64,678,286 29	64,678.

Note. Dans les écritures de la direction générale de la comptabilité chacun des comptes ci-dessus énoncés est détaillé au moyen de développements spéciaux selon la méthode a...

on générale patrimoniale.　　　　　　　　　　　　　　(Comptes spécifiques)　　　EXERCICE 1880.

L'EXERCICE DU BUDGET								CRÉDITS pour résidus actifs relatifs aux budgets des années précédentes		DÉBITS pour résidus passifs relatifs aux budgets des années précédentes		ESPÈCE, crédits patrimoniaux, matières et passivités diverses A-1			
la construction des chemins de fer				Pour partie d'ordre											
RÉDITS		DÉBITS		CRÉDITS		DÉBITS									
Recettes constatées	Sommes disposées	Sommes payées	Recettes recouvrées	Recettes constatées	Sommes disposées	Sommes payées								
Avoir 11	Doit 15	Avoir 16	Doit 17	Avoir 18	Doit 19	Avoir 20	Doit 21	Avoir 22	Doit 23	Avoir 24	Doit 25	Avoir 26
....	....	....	....	....	....	....	....	211,519,941.10	283,384,749.19	....	7,318,306,801.71	....
....	....	....	....	....	....	....	....	....	....	....	23,700,420.41	....
....	....	....	....	....	....	....	....	....	....	....	41,940,417.23	....
67,755,713.30	....	....	....	....	....	....	....	....	....	....	67,755,713.30	....
....	....	....	....	90,883,109.32	....	....	....	....	....	....	90,883,109.32	....
....	....	....	....	175,017.76	....	....	....	....	....	....	....	....
....	....	....	....	....	....	....	....	....	....	....	81,614,353.64	....
....	....	....	....	....	....	....	....	....	....	....	64,678,286.29	....
....	67,987,158.88	....	....	....	....	....	....	....	....	....	67,987,158.88	....
....	....	....	....	....	90,883,109.32	....	....	....	....	....	90,883,109.32	....
....	....	....	....	....	....	....	12,231,415.83	....	....	....	....	....
....	....	....	....	....	....	....	....	....	10,308,413.56	....	....	....
....	....	....	69,565,537.85	....	....	....	....	....	....	....	....	1,297,308,043.72
....	....	....	....	....	....	....	78,191,607.74	....	....	....	....	78,191,607.74
....	....	90,115,045.17	....	....	....	69,363,117.36	....	....	....	....	1,211,356,330.57	....
....	....	....	....	....	....	....	....	....	....	173,257,370.04	173,257,370.04	....
....	....	....	....	....	....	....	....	....	....	....	....	217,295,547.62
....	....	....	....	....	....	....	....	....	....	....	267,361,519.83	....
....	....	....	....	....	....	....	....	....	....	....	43,898,368.55	....
....	....	....	....	....	....	....	....	....	....	....	....	28,785,227.74
....	....	....	....	....	....	....	....	....	....	....	111,586.19	....
67,755,713.30	67,987,158.88	30,115,045.17	69,565,537.85	91,058,127.08	90,883,109.32	69,363,117.36	90,423,023.57	211,519,941.10	283,384,749.19	183,565,783.60	9,238,571,636.65	1,936,683,312.95
....	....	37,872,113.71	21,492,589.23	....	....	21,519,991.96	121,096,917.53	....	....	99,818,965.59	....	7,281,768,303.70
67,755,713.30	67,987,158.88	67,987,158.88	91,058,127.08	91,058,127.08	90,883,109.32	90,883,109.32	211,519,941.10	211,519,941.10	283,384,749.19	283,384,749.19	9,238,571,636.65	9,238,571,636.65

....compte *Espèce, crédits patrimoniaux, matières et passivités diverses* - (25ᵐᵉ et 26ᵐᵉ colonne) que l'on exemplifie en **A-1**.

13

but merely a transformation of assets. At the bottom of the journal is the summary of the fiscal period.

The permutation column is the posting medium to the *svolgimenti*. Only one schedule is shown here, on page 118. Actually Cerboni used nine of them.[58]

This is not a satisfactory exposition of the system of logismography; all that is attempted is to set forth in skeleton form the mechanics of this amazing system.

Logismography lasted as long as Cerboni remained in the post of accountant general. As soon as he vacated his position, logismography was found to be too complicated to be maintained, and in 1893 it was quietly dropped for a system akin to double entry.[59]

BESTA AND MODERN PRACTICE

With Besta, modern accountancy began in Italy. The Venetian school of thought which he represented assumed leadership with the overthrow of Cerboni's logismography, and today his disciples hold the field undisputed.

His system needs no explanation, for it is the same double-entry system used in modern countries, and is the theme of many textbooks.

Fabio Besta emphasized the history and evolution of accounting practice, and in this he provided an example which has been too infrequently followed. Clearly a true perspective and appreciation of accountancy can only be obtained by study of its origin and gradual development. It is disconcerting that many accountants and students have no inkling of bookkeeping's ancient lineage.

NOTES

[1] Bariola. Op. cit., p. 441. "*Giuseppe Pecchio (nel Saggio Storico dell'amministrazione finanziaria dell'ex regno d'Italia dal 1802 al 1814) dice che i conti che pure ogni anno uscivano alla luce in Francia sull'amministrazione delle finanze sia nella precisione sia nel dettaglio e nelle osservazioni, non sostenevano il paragone di quelli del ministero italiano. E. Napoleone I, infatti, nelle sua privata corrispondenza col Beauharnais, lodava i Ragionieri italiani che facevano camminare l'azienda del Tesoro con tal ordine, che a mala pena si poteva introdurre in Francia.*"

[2] Besta. Op. cit., vol. 2, p. 477. "*E proprio la condizione caratteristica essenziale di tali scritture è questa, di considerare i fatti della gestione quali introiti e pagamenti e di classificarli, avuto riguardo a questa distinzione, in registri e in conti o rubriche di entrata e di uscita. Il non accennare negli articoli dei giornali che ad addebitamenti o ad accreditamenti, come suol farsi nelle altre scritture semplici, e l'aggiunta di scritture per i movimenti delle materie a quelle finanziarie, ne sono le caratteristiche esteriori.*"

[3] Bariola. Op. cit., vol. 2, chap. 17.

Ponti, Maria Pasolini. *Sommario della storia d'italia* (Paravia, Torino, 1928), chap. 17.

[4] Bariola. Op. cit., part 2, pp. 457–458.

[5] Besta. Op. cit., vol. 2, p. 357.

Gasperoni, Fulvio. *La professione di ragioniere in italia* (Milano, Esperia, 1935), chap. 6, pp. 51–54.

[6] Besta. Op. cit., vol. 2, pp. 357–358.

Gasperoni. Op. cit., p. 54.

Bariola. Op. cit., p. 515.

[7] Besta. Op. cit., vol. 2, p. 358.

Gasperoni. Op. cit., p. 53.

[8] Paciolo. Op. cit., chap. 12. ". . . *per eo cavedale s'intende tutto il tuo Corpo di facoltà presente*" *e per la cassa* "*la tua propria overo borsica.*" In the summary of the treatise appears — "*farai creditore al tuo conto (il cavedale), cioè te medesimo.*"

[9] Ibid. Chap. 23. ". . . *de l'ordine et modo a saper tenere un conto da bottega. . . . De tutte le robbe che tu vi (mnella bottega) metterai a dì per dì farala debitrice e li toi libri . . . e fa tua imaginatione che questa bottega sia una persona debitrice di quel tanto, che li dai o per lei spendi in tutti li modi. E così per l'averso di tutto quello che ne cavi e recevi farala creditrice comme se fosse un debitore che ti pagasse a parte . . . E molti sono che a li suoi libri fanno debitore il principale che lì attende a ditta bottega, benchè questo non se possa debitamente senza voluntà di quel tale . . .*"

[10] Besta. Op. cit., vol. 2, p. 358.

Gasperoni. Op. cit., p. 52.

[11] Flori. Op. cit., *Libro doppio domestico*, p. 8. "*I debiti ancora e i crediti che si scrivono nei libri . . . non solo appartengono a persone, ma ancora a cose supposte o sia inanimate, come sono nel libro dei mercanti, le loro mercantie, e nel domestico i granari, le cantine, e in tutti la cassa. E queste si chiamano cose supposte o surrogate, perchè nella scrittura tengono luogo di tante persone. Come, per cagion d'esempio, la cassa è come un depositario dei nostri danari e perciò quando ci mettiamo denari gliene diamo debito, come se fusse persona che ce ne avesse a render conto, et all'incontro quando ne leviamo gliene diamo credito come faremmo appunto col depositario quando ce lo restituisse* ". . . *perchè si mettono in luoghi di persone depositarie di quelle cose, e si trattano e maneggiano come se fossero tante persone.*"

[12] Besta. Op. cit., vol. 2, p. 359.

[13] Manzoni. Op. cit., *Quaderno Doppio*, chap. 14. ". . . *per le cose vive, qui s'intende ogni creatura animata; et per le cose morte s'intende robbe over ogni altra cosa.*"

[14] Besta. Op. cit., vol. 2, p. 363.

[15] Dégrange's theory appeared in 1795 in his book, *La tenue des livres rendue facile, ou Nouvelle méthode d'enseignement de la tenue des livre en single et double partie* (Paris, Hocquart, 1795).

[16] Giraudeau. *La banque rendue facile* (Lyons, Regnault, 1769), p. 2.

[17] Dégrange. Op. cit. "*La tenue des livres ou nouveau traité de comptabilité générale*"; p. 6, ". . . *pour se faire une idée de ces comptes, il ne faut voir en eux que ceux du négociant dont on tient les livres, et il faut concevoir que débiter l'un de ces comptes, c'est débiter le négociant lui même sous le nom de ce compte en particulier.*"

[18] Ibid. ". . . *en débitant la personne . . . qui reçoit, ou le compte de l'objeҫt que l'on reçoit; et en créditant . . . la personne qui fournit ou le compte de l'objeҫt que l'on fournit.*"

[19] Besta. Op. cit., vol. 2, pp. 365–366.

Gasperoni. Op. cit., p. 54.

Bariola. Op. cit., part 2, pp. 431–433.

[20] Francesco Villa. *Elementi di amministrazione e contabilità* (Pavia, Bizzoni, 1853), pp. 163–251.

Bariola. Op. cit., part 2, p. 463.

[21] Vannier, Hippolyte. *Traité des tenues de livres* (Paris, Hachete, 1854), "*Tous ces noms de comptes doivent être regardes comme des personifications représentant les employes de la maison. Il faut entendre par marchandises les commis préposés pour reçevoir et livrer les marchandises; par caisse le caissier chargés des encaissements et des payements; par effets a reçevoir celui qui tient le portefeuille des effets actifs; par effets à payer celui qui constate sur un carnet d'écheances la sortie et la rentrée des effets passifs; par mobilier, agencement, frais*

de premier établissement et fonds de commerce, ceux qui doivent rendre compte de ces différentes valeurs.''

[22] Besta. Op. cit., vol. 2, pp. 369–370.

[23] Marchi, Francesco. *I cinquecontisti* (1867), p. 44. *"Per me i conti, qualunque sia la loro intestazione, devonsi ritenere tutti personali e tutti reali, essendo persone i capitalisti o il capitalista dell'azienda, persone coloro che prendono in consegna le mercanzie e il denaro di essa, e persone coloro che ci sono in corrispondenza, tutte le quali (persone) sono realmente debitrici per quanto hanno in dare e creditrici per quanto hanno in avere dell'Azienda.*

[24] Ibid. Pp. 98–99. *"Nelle aziende le più in grande, e quelle sociali specialmente, vi si distinguono in generale quattro qualità di persone che vi hanno interesse od azione, e sono: i consegnatari o coloro i quali prendono in consegna le merci e il denaro, i corrispondenti o coloro con i quali si fanno gli affari a dilazione; il proprietario o colui che fornisce le sostanze che costituiscono l'azienda ed a conto del quale va la medesima; e finalmente il gerente o colui che la dirige e l'amministra responsabilmente.''*

[25] Ibid. P. 196. *"In quelle aziende ove non siano persone diverse dal proprietario, il gerente, il cassiere, il magazziniere, ed altri consegnatari . . . e il proprietario stesso che riveste . . . di ognuno di essi funzionari il carattere, e facendone le veci, ne ha pure i conti della indole di quelli propri de' funzionari medesimi.''*

[26] Ibid. P. 100. *"Addebitare chi riceve un valore o chi di un valore divien debitore, ed accreditare chi lo da o chi ne diviene creditore.''*

[27] Besta. Op. cit., vol. 2, pp. 372–373.
  Gasperoni. Op. cit., pp. 54–55.
  Bariola. Op. cit., part 2, pp. 471–476.

[28] Cerboni, Giuseppe. *Prima saggi di logismografia* (Roma, Botta, 1872), p. 14. *"Non vi possono essere che conti veri e vivi, cioè che attribuiscano a persone veri debiti e crediti, e non conti morti, conti di commodo, conti artificiali che riguardano una quiddità o un'astrazione, sia amministrativa, sia computistica, sia economica.''*

[29] Ibid. Axioms 2 and 3, p. 14. *"Se il proprietario amministra l'azienda da se stesso riveste la doppia qualità di proprietario e di amministratore . . . Se l'amministratore, all'incarico della direzione degli affari dell'azienda, e di darne ragione, aggiungesse pur quello di custodirne materialmente la sostanza, vestirebbe due qualità quella di amministratore, e quella di agente consegnatario.''*

[30] Ibid. Axiom 5, p. 14. *"Il proprietario, amministri o no l'azienda, è di fatto il creditore della sua sostanza, e il debitore delle passività di lei inverso gli agenti e corrispondenti.''*

[31] Cerboni. *Rudimenti di logismografia*, p. 1.

[32] Cerboni. *Primi saggi*, p. 14. *"Il credito del proprietario corrisponde al debito degli agenti e dei corrispondenti, e viceversa il credito di costoro corrisponde al debito del proprietario . . . L'amministratore tiene la bilancia del dare e dell'avere tra il proprietario da una parte, e gli agenti e corrispondenti dall'altra.''*

[33] Cerboni. *Discorso pronunciato il 1 marzo 1876 all'accademia dei ragionieri in Firenze*, p. 16. *"Qualunque scrittura contabile devesi . . . cominciare impostando due conti . . . uno pel proprietario, l'altro per gli agenti e corrispondenti, conti che debbono sempre bilanciare fra di loro, cosicchè l'avere del proprietario sia constantemente uguale al dare degli agenti e dei corrispondenti, e viceversa il dare dell'uno sia sempre reciprocamente eguale all'avere degli altri.''*

[34] Besta. Op cit., vol. 2, pp. 376–382.
  Gasperoni. Op. cit., pp. 55–56.
  Bariola. Op. cit., part 2, pp. 493–507.

[35] Besta. Op. cit., vol. 2, p. 291. *"Adunque ha da potersi in ogni istante aver notizie speditamente del denaro che è in cassa, dello stato dei crediti che l'azienda ha verso ciascuno dei suoi debitori, delle condizioni in cui trovansi i singoli poderi, dei frutti che danno i capitali attivi delle varie classi, delle somme disponibili per ogni voto del bilancio, e via dicendo. Ed è palese a chicchessia che la rapida e sicura ricerca di simile notizie non si può avere se le scritture che serban di memoria dei mutamenti avvenuti in ciascuno di codesti oggetti non si raccolgono insieme in un medesimo luogo. Ciò premesso ciascuna accolta di scritture riferendosi ad un oggetto determinato costituisce ciò che dice un conto, una partita o una rubrica.''*

[36] Ibid. Part 2, p. 292. *"Dalle cose discorse segue che il conto può definirsi: una serie di scritture riguardanti un oggetto determinato, commensurabile e mutabile, e avente per ufficio di serbar memoria della condizione e misura di tale oggetto in un dato istante e dei mutamenti che va subendo, in maniera da poter rendere ragione dello stato di cotesto oggetto in un tempo quale si voglia."*

[37] Ibid. Part 2, pp. 291–401.

Gasperoni. Op. cit., pp. 56–60.

[38] Besta. Op. cit., vol. 3, pp. 226–227.

[39] Paciolo. Op. cit., *Summa*, chap. 11. *"Sappi che di tutte le partite che tu harai poste in lo giornale al quaderno grande te ne convien sempre fare doi, cioè una in dare e l'altra in havere . . . chiamar la carta dove sia quella del suo creditore . . . chiamar la carta di quella dove sia el suo debitore . . . E in questo modo sempre vengono incatenate tutte le partite del ditto quaderno grande, nel quale non si deve metter cosa in dare che quella ancora non si ponga in havere. E così non si deve mettere cosa in havere che ancora quella medesima con suo amontare non si metta in dare. E di qua nasci poi el bilancio che del libro si fa nel suo saldo, tanto convien che sia il dare quanto l'avere."*

[40] Manzoni. *Quaderno doppio*, chap. 11. *". . . più che ad ogn'altra parte debbe attendere, perchè invero qui consiste tutta la difficultà de l'arte, in saper discernere in ciascuna facenda qual sia esso debitore e creditore."*

[41] De La Porte. *La Science des négocians et teneurs de livres*, pp. 77–78. *". . . tenir les livres a parties doubles . . . C'est d'elles dont se servent presque tous les négocians et marchands qui font de grosses affairs, et qui veulent les tenir en bon ordre parce qu'elle embrasse et renferme tout."*

[42] Villa. *Elementi d'amministrazione*, p. 266. *"Le scopo principale della tenuta dei registri a scrittura doppia è quello di rimediare alle imperfezioni del metodo a scrittura semplice . . . Per rimediare a questa mancanza si è in massima trovato opportuno di aggiungere alle partite di deposito ed individuali (non determinate in numero che dalla natura dell'azienda) tre altre partite le quali noi chiameremo riassuntive appunto perchè sono destinate a riassumere le nozioni sparse negli altri conti."*

[43] Besta. Op. cit., vol. 3, pp. 227–232.

[44] Crippa, Lodovico Giuseppe. *La scienza dei conti*, 1838, Chap. 3.

Besta. Op. cit., vol. 3, p. 234.

[45] Besta. Op. cit., vol. 3, pp. 234–236.

Vincenzo Gitti. *La scrittura doppia e le sue forme*, p. 12.

[46] Dégrange. *Tenue des livres rendue facile*, pp. 6–10. *". . . Il y en a cinq principaux (comptes) sans lesquels il est impossible de tenir les livres en parties doubles, d'une manière qui embrasse la totalité des affaires d'un négociant . . . L'usage des comptes généraux étant bien conçu, toute la science de la tenue des livres consiste à savoir passer écriture sur un registre de toutes les opérations de commerce que l'on fait, jour par jour, à mesure que elles ont lieu, en débitant la personne qui reçoit, le compte de l'objet que l'on reçoit; et en creditant dans le même article la personne qui fournit ou le compte de l'objet que l'on fournit."*

[47] Marchi. Op. cit., p. 100. *"Or dal tenersi conto ai corrispondenti, ai consegnatari, ed al proprietario dell'azienda, viene a costituirsi quel sistema completo, che fu detto a partita doppia, per lo scriversi due volte la partita, cioè l'una a debito di uno di quegli individui, l'altra a credito di un altro di essi, essendochè il valore della partita di cui devesi prendere scrittura non possa essere ricevuto dall'uno che non sia dato dall'altro, e non possa maturarsi a debito dell'uno senza che si maturi a credito dell'altro fra i detti individui . . . Addebitare chi riceve un valore o di un valore divien debitore, e accreditare chi lo da e ne divien creditore."*

[48] Besta. Op. cit., vol. 3, pp. 239–252.

[49] Ibid. Part 3, pp. 7–40.

[50] Ibid. Vol. 3, pp. 226–271.

[51] Degrange, Edmond. *Supplément à la tenue des livres rendue facile.* *"Je dois cette méthode à la multiplicité de mes occupations et au besoin d'abreger les écritures relatives à mes affaires . . . Je me servais . . . de cette méthode pour mon usage particulier, sans y attacher une grande importance, lorsqu'on m'apporta celle de M. Jones (Intitulé: La*

tenue des livres simplifiée) pour la quelle il a obtenue en Angleterre un brevet d'invention. La superiorité que je crus apercevoir dans la mienne, m'y fit, alors seulement, attacher quelque prix, et me décida à la publier."

[52] Besta. Op. cit., vol. 3, pp. 421–444.
[53] Riva, Michele. *La partita doppia e l'amministrazione dello stato, delle provincie e dei comuni* (1869).
[54] Bariola. Op. cit., part 2, pp. 493–507.
[55] Cerboni. *"Primi saggi . . ."*
[56] Ibid. P. 14.

"I. Every business organization consists of one or more companies, each with a proprietor or administrator to whom the firm belongs, either outright or as an agent. To manage a firm one has to enter into business relationships with employees and debtors and creditors.

1st corollary: One or more individuals united into a society may be the proprietors of a firm.
2nd corollary: The administrator of the firm, if not the proprietor himself, will always be a representative of his, with powers equal to his as regards third persons.
3rd corollary: The proprietor or representative has the right of management of the firm.
"II. It is one thing to own a firm, and another to manage it.
Corollary: If the proprietor manages the firm himself, he assumes the double characteristic of proprietor and administrator.
"III. It is one thing to manage a firm, and another to be responsible for assets assigned to one's care.
Corollary: If the administrator of the firm was also responsible for specific assets placed in his care, he assumed the double characteristic of administrator and consignee (employee).
"IV. A debtor is not created without simultaneous creation of a creditor, and vice-versa.
Corollary: Every transaction of the firm must be registered in debit and credit.
"V. Whether or not the proprietor manages the firm, he is nevertheless the creditor of its assets and the debtor of its liabilities; the reverse is true of agents and debtors and creditors.
1st corollary: A credit of the proprietor corresponds to the debit of agents and debtors and creditors, while a credit of one of the latter corresponds to a debit of the proprietor.
2nd corollary: The administrator holds the balance of debits and credits between the proprietor, on the one side, and the agents and debtors and creditors, on the other side.
3rd corollary: An administrator cannot be a debtor or creditor of the firm without being a consignee or a correspondent.
"VI. The debit or credit of a proprietor varies only because of losses or profits, i.e., increases or decreases of the capital invested by the proprietor.
Corollary: Permutations of elements constituting the capital of a firm, or a passage of a sum from one agent or correspondent to another, if the sum of the permutation or passage is identical, cannot modify the net worth of the proprietor or the aggregate total of agents and correspondents."

[57] See example on pages 114 and 118.
[58] Cerboni. *L'importance d'unifier les études de la comptabilité.*
 I. Schedule A. The State — the general administration of its patrimony.
 II. Schedule A-1. Miscellaneous credits of the patrimony, miscellaneous liabilities.
 III. Schedule A-2. The State — the general economic administration.
 IV. Schedule B. Agents and correspondents — the general administration of the patrimony.
 V. Schedule B-1. Consignees of current assets.
 VI. Schedule C. The State — estimated and realized receipts.
 VII. Schedule D. Government officials — estimated and realized receipts.
 VIII. Schedule E. The State — estimated and realized disbursements.
 IX. Schedule F. Government officials — estimated and realized disbursements.
[59] Bariola. Op. cit., part 2, pp. 493–533.
 Besta. Op. cit., vol. 3, pp. 469–589.
 Cerboni. *Sur l'importance d'unifier les études de la comptabilité.*

PART III

THE FUNCTIONAL DEVELOPMENT
OF DOUBLE ENTRY

THE LEDGER

THE JOURNAL

FINANCIAL STATEMENTS

Chapter VIII

THE FUNCTIONAL DEVELOPMENT
OF DOUBLE ENTRY

SO FAR the evolution of double entry in Italy has been traced by a study of the actual books of account used by mercantile and industrial houses, as well as governmental authorities, at Genoa, Florence, and Venice during the fourteenth and fifteenth centuries, supplemented by a review of the slowly developing literature on accounting theory and procedure. The object has been to show how double entry first came into being and gradually assumed the nature of a well defined system of bookkeeping. No attempt has been made to treat individually and in detail the various procedures and devices which go to make up the system of double entry. In this chapter double entry will be considered exclusively from a functional viewpoint. The ledger, the journal, and the principal financial statements will each be reviewed in turn, showing how they came into use and gradually assumed their present form and purpose.

THE LEDGER

Aside from crude memorandum books, the ledger is the first double-entry record to appear; the journal was developed at a much later date. The earliest ledgers are those of the *Massari del Comune di Genova* (stewards of the Commune of Genoa) of 1340, the Datini ledgers of Florence, and those of the merchants of Venice. An example from each of these ledgers will be shown.

From the Massari ledger: [1]

LA COLONNA PIPER *carte* LXXIII

MCCCXXXX, *die* VII *Marcii*
Piper Centenaria LXXX *debent nobis pro Venciguerra Imperiali valent nobis in* VIII *et sunt pro libris* xxiiij *sol.* v *pro centenario*

lib. MDCCCCXXXX
Censarius Luchas Donatus

MCCCXXXX, *die* XII *marcii*
Recepimus in vendea de centaries dicti piperis in Joanne de Franco de Florentia, el pro eo in racione Cristiani Lomellini, valent nobis in III. *lib.* CCXXVII, *s.* V *et sunt pro lib.* xxij, *sol.* XIIII, *d.* VI *ad numeratum.*

Item die, etc.

Item die, etc.

The familiar paragraph construction of ledger entries, the details of which have been amply discussed in part I, is shown in this example. An account taken from the Datini ledgers (1383) after the lateral accounts had been introduced, illustrates the type of account used in Florence:[2]

C. lxxxxkt:
Nicholò di Francesco e Fratelli di Firenze de'dare a dì xvj di maggio fior. quattrociento d., demo per lui a Messer Banduccio Bonchonti; portò Simone di Francescho a uscita B. ac 132.   *fior. cccc, d.*

C. lxxxxij:
Nicholò di Francesco e Fratelli da Firenze deono avere in dì xiiij di maggio prossimo fior. quatrociento d., i quali gli promettemo a dì viij di Febraio per Piero del Pucci, chatalano; posto adietro in questo ac. 82 Piero d'dare.
fior, cccc, d.

From the Venetian ledgers, taken from Andrea Barbarigo:[3]

MCCCCXXX
Debitori et creditori trati dal libro biancho picholo A deno dar a dì e Zenaro per Andrea Barbarigo che fui de Meser Nicholò chome apar in quello a K. 2 . . . lb. xx, s.   , d.   , p. o

MCCCCXXX
Debitori et creditori controscritti demo aver a dì 2 zenaro per Piero Soranzo fo de ser Antonio apar in questo K. 7 . . .   lb.   , s. xiij, d. x, p. o

These three examples illustrate the earliest forms of ledger entries. The construction of the entry is the same in all instances: the paragraph form, including the title of the account, the date, the nature of the transaction, the title and page reference of the contra debit or credit entry, and finally the total amount appearing at the end of the entry. The first digression from this form of ledger entry occurred in the sixteenth century, when Zuan Antonio Barbarigo and Manzoni introduced consecutive numbers in their cross-index system. This innovation soon began to fall gradually into discard. The following debit entry is quoted from page 20 of Manzoni's *Quaderno*:[4]

129   *Spese di Villa, die dar adì 31 Marzo, a cassa, p. più spese fatte in la mia possession da campo san Piero, per far pinatar, fossalar et altre cose necessarie in quella, da adì po Marzo, per fin questo zorno, come appar in libro di spese di villa, d. 65 g. 10 p.   CI 1.6, s. 10, g. 10 p.*

The number 129 at the beginning of the entry refers to the consecutive numbers of the journal entries and facilitates tracing ledger entries to the journal. The CI at the end of the entry refers to the contra credit entry in the ledger, a device inherited from the early index system.

The next change is the development of the compound journal entry. Flori follows Simon Stevin's lead in advocacy of entries composed of more than one debit and credit element. The system of cross-indexing underwent a corresponding change. Flori ignored the consecutive numbers of Manzoni and Barbarigo, but clung to the cross-reference of contra debits and credits of the ledger. The following debit entry is quoted from page 16 of his *Libro Doppio:* [5]

$$+ \text{ I. Ind. // } 1633.$$

r   *Salarij diversi dare a dì primo di Maggio* ____ 16.
                                                                                   (

      alli detti, per l'ultimo terzo, come in Giornale _____ 00 16 ____
                                                                                                       (

The two zeros at the end of the entry mean that there are more than one credit and that, to avoid repeating the page number of the credits, Flori refers the reader to the journal for the information. The *r* at the beginning of the entry means that it has been checked against the journal entry and found correct.

With the nineteenth century, ledger accounts and entries began to assume a more modern appearance. The following debit account is taken from Luigi Aloardi's book, *Il Ragioniere,* 1817:

Interessi Attivi e Passivi

Dare

1811		
Gennajo 2 A cassa conte per interessi al 5% sopra L130 M. dal 27 febbrajo a tutt'oggi	F° 7 L.	1, 679–16–9
Giugno 6 A Suddetta Conte in saldo sopra L. 40M a tutt'oggi	F° 7 L.	855–55–6
	L.	2, 534–71–9

Interest Income and Expense

Debit

Jan. 3, 1811	Credit cash for interest expense at 5% of L. 130,000 from Feb. 27 to date	p. 7 L.	1, 679–16–9
Jun. 6,	Credit cash in payment of interest on the liquidation of debt of L. 40,000.	p. 7 L.	855–55–6
		L.	2, 534–71–9

A title separate from the entry itself is displayed at the top of the account. Distinct date and money columns are used. Position gradually has taken the place of technical phrases, and the accounts have become more closely knit, a characteristic of twentieth-century accounting. The one feature that did not change was the cross-index system. The accounts bear reference only to contra ledger entries.

In the following year, 1818, Giuseppe Bornaccini introduced a new feature in ledger accounts, as shown by the following debit quoted from his book: [6]

DARE (debit)

1816

Spese a Dazio Consumo (Consumption Tax Expense)	giornale (journal)	maśtro (ledger)	totale (total)	
Dicembre 31 Al Fattore per Dazio pagato (Dec. 31, 1816 Credit agent for tax paid)	66	42	L. 154	59 —

To the old system of cross-indexing, Bornaccini added an additional column for reference to the journal entry. Thus the ledger accounts bear both ledger and journal cross-reference folios.

The ledger account moves closer to its modern synthetic form in Villa's *Contabilità Applicata*. On page 216 of part one of his book, appears the following account:

Dare (dr.) Fol. 5 (p. 5)				Spese per Salari (Salary Expense)			Avere (cr.)	
30	Gennajo	alla cassa per pagate al magazziniero per salario di un mese fol.	2 L. 40 00	31	Gennajo	Dalla cavata per saldo fol.	7 L. 40	00
30	January	Credit cash for a month's salary of warehouse man.	p. 2 L. 40 00	31	January	To profit and loss for balance of account.	p. 7 L. 40	00

The ruling shown here is very close to modern form. Villa did not use the double column for cross-indexing, but adhered to the old system of cross-referencing contra ledger entries.

Fabio Besta constructed his ledger accounts somewhat differently, but he introduced no new feature. The following account is quoted from his book: [7]

(10) *Dare* (dr)   *Spese Generali* (general expenses)   *Avere* (cr) (10)

Data (Date)	Gior. J.	Mas-tro L.					Data (Date)	Gior. J.	Mas-tro L.			
1 Luglio	17	11	A Cassa, spese diverse pagate nel semmestre L.	8,100 00	8,100 00		31 Luglio	23	3	Da spese e rendite, saldo di questo conto L.	8,100 00	8,100 00
1 Jul.	17	11	(Credit cash, for miscella-neous exp. for semester)		L. 8,100 00		31 Jul.	23	3	(To P. & L. for balance of account)		L. 8,100 00

The outstanding characteristic here is the recurrence of Manzoni's old index system. Even though Besta ushers in the modern era of accountancy, he still clings to the old use of consecutive numbers for tracing ledger entries to the journal and of cross-referencing contra ledger entries, necessitating two columns for this purpose in ledger accounts. At the turn of the century the modern system of cross indexing was not as yet known in Italy. In all other respects, however, the ledger account was in modern form. The long analytical paragraph entries had given way to modern synthetic entries. The use of technical phrases to distinguish debits from credits had been supplanted by the use of position for the same purpose. A left position had come to indicate a debit and a right position a credit.

THE JOURNAL

The earliest journal so far discovered, that of Andrea Barbarigo, bears the date of 1430. Before that time, one ledger, supplemented by numerous memorandum books, constituted the usual set of books. Even after the introduction of the journal, memorandum books had an important rôle to play. Paciolo rated them on a par with the ledger and the journal. It was only in the sixteenth century that they began to decline in importance, and thereafter they gradually dropped out of bookkeeping altogether.

The purpose of memorandum books was twofold: they served as diary books for listing transactions as they occurred, in the particular coinage they happened to be dealt in, whether domestic or foreign, and they were also used for segregating transactions of one kind, such as household, labor, or farm expenses.

Originally, the journal served as an intermediary between the memorandum books used by all clerks transacting business and the ledger; transactions noted in these memorandum books were recorded in the journal with the amounts converted into domestic coinage, preparatory to posting them to the ledger. An example is quoted below from Barbarigo's journal: [8]

$\frac{18}{7}$ *In Christi nomine in MCCCCXXX a dì 2 zenaro in Venexia.*
Per cassa de contanti A ser Francesco Balbi e fradelli contadi da ser Nicholò de Bernardo e fradelli e ser Matio e ser Zan de Garzoni per nome de ser Armano per resto de zaferan duc. 4, g. 3, p. 16 val.
                                                            lb., s. viij, d. iij, p. 16.

$\frac{5}{14}$ *1430 adì 8 zenaro*
Per ser Nofrio decalzi de Lucha A ser Francesco Balbi e fradelli per lo bancho i de contar per mi.   *lb. iij, s.   , d.   , p. o.*

The entries here are constructed in the usual paragraph form. The debit and credit are distinguished by the two prepositions: *Per*, meaning debit, and *A*, meaning credit. The date is set at the top of the entry and the fraction on the side shows the ledger-folio postings, the numerator being the debit posting and the denominator the credit posting. An essential characteristic of the early journal is the simple entry. A transaction involving more than one debit and credit element would be split into as many entries as there were elements. The paragraph form hindered the use of compound journal entries.

Manzoni's journal entries differed somewhat from those of Barbarigo's early journal. Entry number 129 is quoted from Manzoni's *Giornale*: [9]

                              1540 adì 31 mazo
129   $\frac{20}{1}$ *P Spese de Villa // A Cassa, per più spese fatte in la mia possession da campo San Piero, per far piantar, fossalar et altre cose necessarie in quella, da di po marzo prossimo passato, fin questo zorno, come appar in libro de spese di villa, in tutto d. 65, g. 10*   *l. 6, s. 10, g. 10. p.*

Manzoni used consecutive numbers for his journal entries in addition to the fraction. He also used double vertical lines to separate debits from credits, and the letter *P* for the debit, instead of *Per*. The most notable change is the addition of consecutive numbers to the cross-index system. As already mentioned, Manzoni was not the first one to use this device; it had been introduced by Zuan Antonio Barbarigo in 1537.

Almost a century elapsed before the next significant change occurred in the form of the journal — the compound entry, of which the following, taken from page 12 of Flori's journal, is an example: [10]

+Prim. Ind. // 1633

A 30 di Aprile

r   16   *Salarij diversi // alli appresso* ____ *sedici, se li fan buoni anticipata-*
r   o   (

mente per l'ultimo terzo dell'anno presente prima Ind. et a compimento, etc. degl'infrascritti loro salarij, come medico, barbiero, avvocato, procuratore, e sollecitatore respettivamente di questo nostro collegio, cioe A.

r   16   *Dottor Carlo Segni nostro medico* _____ 4 _____
                                            (

r   16   *M. Francesco Nigno nostro barbiero* _____ 2 _____
                                            (

r   17   *Dott. Horatio Archinto nostro Avvocato* _____ 4 _____
                                            (

r   17   *Domenico Tagliaviva nostro Procuratore* _____ 4 _____
                                            (

r   17   *Raffaele Botti nostro Sollecitatore* _____ 2 _____
                                            (
                                        ____ 16 _____ 16 ____

Flori named this type of journal entry *partita collettiva* (compound entry). The phrase *alli appresso* which occurs in the example means "credit the following," referring to the five credit entries listed below. Under the old journal system, five separate entries would have been necessary. This was a great advance toward the modern journal.

The compound entry forced a change in the cross-index system. The zero in the denominator of the fraction indicates that the credits are more than one and are listed below with their ledger folios. The change necessitated in the ledger accounts has already been discussed. Flori ignored Manzoni's consecutive journal numbers.

Flori abandoned the traditional phrases of *Per* and *A* (for and to), and adopted instead *Da* and *A* (from and to). These prepositions, in both cases, respectively stand for "debit" and "credit," but he believes *Da* is more logical than *Per*. However, he omits *Da* completely from his journal entries, and uses it only in the credit entries of the ledger, indicating their contra debit entries, as is shown in the following credit to the cash account:[11]

                                                           8

r   *Havere a 2 dì Gennaro* ____ *1.6 dalla Calzoleria* _____ 1.6 __
                            ((

The journal had advanced no further than this at the beginning of the nineteenth century. An example taken from page 31 of Niccolò D'Anastasio's book *La scrittura doppia ridotta a scienza*, published in 1803, shows how little it differed from Flori's journal entries:

4 Gennaro 1800

____1 *Da Cassa // A Capitale L. 66,200 poste nella medesima oggi che*
       cominciò a fare il negoziante   *L. 66,200—*
_____
2____

Jan. 4, 1800

____1 Debit cash | | credit capital of the owner.   L. 66,200—
_____
2____

The only difference is that D'Anastasio uses the preposition *Da* in the journal entry, whereas Flori reserved it for the ledger entries.

Francesco Villa, writing in 1840, began to break away from the ancient form of journal entry. An example, quoted from page 199, volume 1, of his book, *La contabilità applicata*, illustrates the differences:

1838 3 Ottobre

Cassa lire 2000 a Giovanni $\frac{7}{27}$ *lire 2000*
    per tante pagate per tal titolo

October 3, 1838

Debit cash and credit Giovanni $\frac{7}{27}$ lire 2000
    for cash received

First of all, the debit and credit are placed on a single line with the explanation below, thus departing from the traditional paragraph form. Furthermore, vertical lines do not separate the debit from the credit, and only the preposition *a* for the credit is used. The fraction indicating the ledger folios is placed next to the money column, this position being in agreement with modern bookkeeping practice.

Ilario Tarchiani, in 1868, described a journal which is essentially modern in form. An example from page 54 of his book *Guida teorico-practica sulle scritture comparate ossia per bilancio* shows how far the journal had progressed since publication of Villa's book in 1840:

GIORNALE A DOPPIA COLONNA (Journal with Double Column)

Data			DESCRIZIONE DELLE PARTITE (Description)	DEBITI (dr.)		CREDITI (cr.)	
	MESE (DATE)	(L.F.)					
1	Gennaio (Jan.)		———— 1. ————				
			Acquisto di metri 10,000 panno a L. 9 il metro (Purchased 10,000 meters of cloth @ 1.9 per meter)				
		1	Mer. in Monte pel panno acquiſt. L. (Purchase of merchandise — cloth)	90,000	00		
			Ugo Tarchiani per la valuta sudetta L.			90,000	00
		5.	(Ugo Tarchiani for the above value)				
			. . . .				
11	"		———— 8. ————				
			Per l'acquiſto di due vacche come da ordine ecc. (For the purchase of two cows)	480	00	480	00
		17/2	Gilli Pietro colonno in C ᵗᵒ ſtime vive a cassa in monte (dr. Pietro and cr. cash for the coſt of cows)				

Here are combined characteriſtics of both the ancient and the modern journal.
It is ruled in a modern fashion with separate debit and credit columns, but the
ledger-folio column and the conſtruction of the entries ſtill contain characteriſtics
of the old journal. One peculiarity is the placing of the explanation at the
beginning of the entry. The firſt entry above shows the debit and credit in the
correct position: both are on separate lines and in the correct columns. The
ledger-folio number ſtill retains, however, the old fraction line; when the
number is above the line it is a debit, when it is below it is a credit. In the second
entry Tarchiani reverts to the old form: the debit and credit are not placed on
separate lines, and the old fraction appears in the ledger-folio column.

Fabio Beſta developed a journal in a form peculiarly his own, as an example,
(p. 136), quoted from volume 3, page 119, of his book *Laragioneria*, shows.
The two money columns are not divided into debit and credit columns, but into
a detailed column and a total column. The debits and credits are diſtinguished by
the two cross-index columns at the left and by the conſtruction of the entry. The
debit title is placed at the left and the credit title at the right. Whenever there are
more than one of either debits or credits, the phrase *a diversi*, meaning "to
several," is used, and the detailed accounts are liſted below the explanation.
This ſtructure is modeled closely upon the compound-entry form. Beſta does
not use the fraction in his cross-indexing, but the two ledger-folio columns do
not differ materially from the fraction. The left column is reserved for debit
poſtings and the right column for credit poſtings, whereas in the fraction the
nominator was reserved for debit and the denominator for credit poſtings. The

14	11	12. — m — *MUTUI ATTIVI* (loans of funds at interest) *a CASSA* (cr. cash) *Somme sborsate per mutui*.................L. (cash paid for loans at interest)		50,000	00	50,000	00
	11	16. — q — *CASSA* (cash) *a diversi* (cr., several) *Esazione di rendita del semestre in corso* (income for the six months)					
	4	*A INTERESSI, maturati nel semestre*.............L. (cr. interest matured during the six months)		1,000	00		
	6	*A FITTI, decorsi nel semestre corrente*...............L. (cr. rent income collected during the six months)		2,600	00	3,600	00
	11	17. — r — *Diversi* (several) *A CASSA* (cr. cash) *Somme pagate per ispese e carichi* (cash paid for expenses)					
	10	*SPESE GENERALI, spese del semestre*............L. (general expenses for the semester)		8,100	00		
	9	*IMPOSTE E TASSE, imposte del semestre*..........L. (Duties and taxes for the semester)		2,200	00	10,300	00

only difference seems to be that the fraction line has changed its position from horizontal to vertical. In addition, Besta uses Manzoni's cumbersome system of consecutive numbers for journal entries; these numbers are placed in the left-hand corner of the entry. The letters of the alphabet in the middle of the entries indicate the place of the date.

Besta does not embody in his journal the improvements which he so skilfully effected in all other sections of accounting. In fact, his journal in some respects actually retrogressed from Tarchiani's journal.

FINANCIAL STATEMENTS

The evolution of financial statements is difficult to trace. The earliest balance-sheets known to exist are those constructed by the Florentine merchants of the fourteenth and fifteenth centuries. A liberal translation of a *bilancio* (balance-sheet), drawn from Datini's records and already discussed earlier in the book,[12] is given on the following page. The construction of the *bilancio* is simple. The assets are listed in total, and the total liabilities, including the capital of the two partners, are listed underneath. The difference between these two totals is the net profit for the period, which is divided equally among the two partners.

	Fiornini	Soldi	Denari
Merchandise and other assets in stores on Sep. 27, 1368	3,141	23	4
Accounts Receivable	6,518	23	4
	9,660	22	8
Total liabilities including the capital accounts of the two partners, Francesco and Toro	7,838	18	9
Net profit for the fiscal period	1,822	3	11

The net profit is divided equally among the two partners:

		Fiornini	Soldi	Denari
Francesco	½ of profits	911	2	—
Toro	½ of profits	911	1	11
Total profits distributed		1,822	3	11

The outstanding characteristic of this *bilancio* is its use as a statement for determining profits and losses; the profit-and-loss statement had not yet been devised. This *bilancio* seems to be the outcome of Florentine partnerships. An equable division of profits and losses among the partners was imperative, and the *bilancio* was developed for this specific purpose. The fact that later Venetian writers, who limited themselves to accounting for single ownerships, did not mention the *bilancio*, as a balance-sheet, strengthens this supposition.

The religious orders of the sixteenth and seventeenth centuries also contributed to the development of financial statements. The superiors of the monastic institutions required that the accounts be reviewed four times a year. Don Angelo Pietra and Fra Lodovico Flori, writing respectively in 1586 and 1633, made extensive inquiries on the subject. Both authors agreed that the best method was to submit only three accounts, instead of the whole ledger, which, taken together, would faithfully reflect in a concise form the year's operations. They chose the following accounts: *la spesa e entrata generale* (profit-and-loss account), *l'esito generale di quest'anno* (the balance account, which was in effect a balance-sheet), and the *monastero nostro* (the capital account). These three accounts were not presented in statement form, but were merely copied from the ledger and submitted to the abbot in their account form. Both authors affirm that a proper exposition of financial affairs can be accomplished only at the end of the year, when the yearly operations of the monastery are completed. The interesting point is the development of a profit-and-loss statement, even if still presented in its account form. The fact that monastic institutions did not belong to a proprietor, but to a religious order, necessitated the development

RENDICONTO

D'amministrazione della sostanza del Sig. Giovanni Rossi, desunto dal registro precedente.

ATTIVO (cr.)

Rimanenza attiva al 1 gennaio 1836......			L. 168,344	00
RENDITA				
Interessi attivi.....	L.	755	62	
Prodotto lordo di fitti....		1,675	00	
„ „ di beni in economia.....		220	00	
Prodotto lordo di lavori stradali.....		76,000	00	
Utile sull'esito di frumento e riso......		190	00	
quota di livello corrispondente ad un bimestre....		333	33	
Somma la rendita.....	L. 79,173	95	79,173	95
Maggior valore verificatosi nel diretto dominio all'atto della vendita.....			3,334	00
Somma l'attività...			L. 250,851	95

PASSIVO (dr.)

Rimanenza passiva al 1 gennajo 1836			L. 2,475	00
SPESA				
Interessi passivi.....	L.	33	77	
Spese inerenti a prodotti di fitto.....		134	45	
Spese inerenti ad amministrazione economica di fondi.....		597	20	
Spese inerenti a lavori stradali.....		74,405	31	
Perdita sull'esito del melgone.....		200	00	
Spese di famiglia.....		1,788	00	
Spesa di negozio.....		630	00	
Somma la spesa.....	L. 77,788	73	77,788	73
Somma la passività..			L. 80,263	73

DIMOSTRAZIONE

	Rimanenza		Annuità		Sopravvenienza		Totale	
Attivo......	L. 168,344	00	L. 79,173	95	L. 3,334	00	L. 250,851	95
Passivo......	2,475	00	77,788	73			80,263	73
Netto......	L. 165,869	00	L. 1,385	22	L. 3,334	00	L. 170,588	22

Attività al 30 aprile 1836......	L. 170,763	22
Passività alla sudetta epoca.....	175	00
Netto, come alla liquidazione......	L. 170,588	22

STATEMENT

Of administration of Giovanni Rossi's capital as taken from the ledger.

CREDITS

Credit capital balance at Jan. 1, 1836.............			L. 168,344	00
——INCOME——				
Interest income.........	L.	755	62	
Gross income rents.....		1,675	00	
" " saving in goods.................		220	00	
Gross income — Roads..		76,000	00	
Profit from wheat and rice................		190	00	
Portion of income belonging to this fiscal period..............		333	33	
Total income........		L. 79,173	95	79,173	95
Increment over cost in price of goods sold.....		3,334	00	3,334	00
Total credits......				L. 250,851	95

DEBITS

Debit capital balance at Jan. 1, 1836..........			L. 2,475	00
——EXPENSES——				
Interest expense.........	L.	33	77	
Expenses attached to rents...............		134	45	
Expenses attached to the administration...........		597	20	
Expenses attached to property...............		74,405	31	
Expenses — Road work loss on (melgone).....		200	00	
Family expenses........		1,788	00	
Business expenses......		630	00	
Total expenses......		L. 77,788	73	77,788	73
Total debits.......				L. 80,263	73

SUMMARY AND LIQUIDATION

	Initial Balances		Profit and loss elements					
			Annual items		Increases		Totals	
Credits.................	L. 168,344	00	L. 79,173	95	L. 3,334	00	L. 250,851	95
Debits..................	2,475	00	77,788	73			80,263	73
Net Balance.............	L. 165,869	00	L. 1,385	22	L. 3,334	00	L. 170,588	22

PROOF

Total assets as of April 30, 1836..............	L. 170,763	22
Total liabilities as of the same date............	175	00
Net worth as shown in the above summary............	L. 170,588	22

of financial statements with fundamentally modern conceptions, in order to exert a measure of control over individual monasteries which lacked the supervision of the single-ownership proprietor.

Financial statements had been discussed by many authors, but it remained for Francesco Villa to make it a central thesis. Villa included a balance account and a profit-and-loss account in his ledger, but then developed a statement including both balance-sheet and profit-and-loss elements, an example of which is shown on pages 138 and 139.[13] This statement is neither a balance-sheet nor a profit-and-loss statement, but is in the nature of a detailed account of Rossi's capital. It begins by stating the initial credit and debit balances of the capital account; the credits are placed on the left-hand side and the debits on the right-hand side. After the initial balances, follow the increases of capital due to income and the decreases due to expenses. The credits and debits are totaled and entered below in a summary schedule, where the net present capital is determined and proved by ascertaining whether it agrees with the net difference between total assets and total liabilities.

Fabio Besta, using the equation, $A - P = C$ (assets − liabilities = capital or net worth) follows in Villa's footsteps and adopts his type of financial statement. As an alternative, however, he recommends the plain account form of financial statement.[14]

In conclusion, it may be stated that Italy, at the turn of the century, though a leader in accounting theory, still adhered to certain antiquated practices. She was still using an outmoded cross-index system, had not as yet adopted the modern form of journal, and had made only a crude beginning in the development of modern financial statements.

NOTES

[1] For translation see p. 8.
[2] For translation see p. 26.
[3] For translation see p. 36.
[4] For translation see p. 61.
[5] For translation see p. 87.
[6] Bornaccini, Giuseppe. *Idee teoriche e Pratiche di Ragioneria, e di doppio giro di Registrazione* (Rimini, Marsoner e Grandi, 2 ed., 1838), p. 18.
[7] Besta. Op. cit., vol. 3, p. 126.
[8] For translation see p. 35.
[9] For translation see p. 61.
[10] For translation see p. 86.
[11] For translation see p. 85.
[12] See chap. 2.
[13] Villa. Op. cit., part 1, p. 252.
[14] Besta. Op. cit., vol. 3, pp. 610–616.

BIBLIOGRAPHY

Bibliography

THE HISTORY OF ACCOUNTING

ALFIERI, VITTORIO: La partita doppia applicata alle scritture delle antiche aziende mercantili veneziane. Torino, ditta G. B. Paravia e comp., 1891.

BARIOLA, PLINIO: Storia della ragioneria italiana premiata al concorso della Societa' storica lombarda.
Parte 1. Storia dell'arithmetica mercantile.
Parte 2. Formazione storica della ragioneria italiana.
Parte 3. La professione.
Milano, Cavalli, 1897.

BENSA, ENRICO: Francesco di Marco da Prato; notizie e documenti sulla mercantura italiana del secolo XIV . . . Milano, Treves, 1928.

BORRELLI DE SERRES, LÉON LOUIS: Compte d'une mission de Prédication pour secours à la Terre Sainte (1265) par le Colonel Borrelli de Serres. Paris, Société de l'histoire de Paris, 1904.

BRAMBILLA, GIUSEPPE: Storia della ragioneria italiana. Milano, Boriglione, 1901.

BROWN, RICHARD: A history of accounting and accountants, ed. and partly written by Richard Brown. Edinburgh, T. C. & E. C. Jack, 1905.

CAMPI, VINCENZO: Il ragioniere.

CECCHERELLI, ALBERTO: Le scritture commerciali nelle antiche aziende fiorentine. Firenze, Lastrucci, 1910.

CHIAUDANO, MARIO: Il più antico rotolo di rendiconti della finanza sabauda (1257–1259). Milano, Miglietta, 1930.

CORSANI, GAETANO: I fondaci e i banchi di un mercante pratese del trecento; contributo alla storia della ragioneria e del commercio, da lettere e documenti inediti. Prato, "La Tipografia", 1922.

DUPONT, ALBERT: Les auteurs comptables du XVI° siècle dans l'empire germanique et les Pay's Bas . . . par M. Albert Dupont . . . Paris, Société de Comptabilité de France, 192–?

DUPONT, ALBERT: Les successeurs de Paciolo en Italie. Paris, Société de Comptabilité de France, 192–?

EDLER, FLORENCE: Glossary of medieval terms of business, Italian Series, 1200–1600. By Florence Edler . . . Cambridge, Mediaeval Academy of America, 1931.

ELDRIDGE, H. J.: The Evolution of the Science of bookkeeping, by H. J. Eldridge . . . London, Institute of bookkeepers, ltd., 1931.

GASPERONI, FULVIO: La professione di ragioniere in Italia . . . da Fulvio Gasperoni . . . Milano, officine grafiche "Esperia", 1935.

LITTLETON, ANANIAS CHARLES: Accounting Evolution to 1900, by A. C. Littleton. New York, N. Y., American Institute Publishing Co., Inc., 1933.

LUCCHINI, ERNESTO: Storia della ragioneria italiana, del . . . Ernesto Lucchini . . . Milano, Amministrazione del periodico "Il ragioniere", 1898.

OPERE ANTICHE DI RAGIONERIA: Milano, Amministrazione del "Monitore dei ragionieri", 1911.

PONTI, MARIA PASOLINI: Sommario della storia d'Italia. Paravia, Torino, 1928.

ROOVER, RAYMOND DE: La Formation et l'Expansion de la Comptabilité à partie double. Paris, Librairie Armand Colin, 1937.

WOOLF, ARTHUR HAROLD: A short history of accountants and accountancy, by Arthur H. Woolf . . . with a bibliography comp. by Cosmo Gordon. London, Gee & Co., ltd., 1912.

CHRONOLOGICAL BIBLIOGRAPHY OF ACCOUNTING

COTRUGLI RAUGEO, BENEDETTO: Della mercatura et del mercante perfetto, libri quattro di M. Benedetto Cotrugli Raugeo, scritti già più di anni CX et hora dati in luce . . . in Venetia, all'Elefante, MDLXXIII (1573). Small treatise on the institutions of commerce. Bookkeeping touched upon briefly and not very well conceived. Important mainly for antedating Paciolo's work by 36 years.

PACIOLO, LUCA: Summa de arithmetica, geometria, proportioni et proportionalità. Venice 1494. Earliest book in existence describing, with great wealth of detail, the Venetian method of double entry. It diffused the knowledge of double entry throughout Europe.

TAGLIENTE, GIOVANNI ANTONIO: Luminario di arithmetica. Venetia 1525. Slender pamphlet on double entry. No new contributions. Far inferior to Paciolo's work.

ANONYMOUS: Opera che insegna a tener conti de libro secondo lo consueto di tutti li lochi della Italia, al modo mercantile . . . Venetia, 1525. Unimportant. Faulty, meager outline of the mechanics of double entry.

ANONYMOUS: Opera che insegna a tener libro doppio et a far partite, e ragion de' banchi, e de mercantie, a riportar le partite, . . . Venetia 1529. Unimportant.

CARDANO, GEROLAMO: Hieronimi C. Cardani medici mediolanensis, practica arithmetice, & mensurandi singularis. In qua que preter alias cōtinentur, versa pagina demonstrabit (Mediolani, Io. Antonins Castellioneus, 1539). Written in Latin; one chapter dedicated to double entry. A highly condensed summary of Paciolo's "Tractatus".

MANZONI, DOMENICO: Quaderno doppio col suo giornale, novamente composto, & diligentissimamente ordinato, secondo il costume di Venetia. Opera a ogni persona utilissima, & molto necessaria. Di Domenico Manzoni, opitergiense . . . (Venetia, Comin de Tridino de Monferrato) 1540. Paciolo's "Tractatus" is followed closely. Merit lies in what was omitted from latter and in the addition of a complete set of double-entry books of high didactic value.

FONTANA, BARTOLOMEO: Ammaestramento novo che insegna a tener libro ordinariamente ad uso di questa città di Venetia, come etiam di tutta l'Italia. 1551. Small pamphlet. Poor summary of Tagliente's already bad work.

CASANOVA, ALVISE: Specchio lucidissimo nel quale si vedono essere diffinito tutti i modi, e ordini de scrittura che si deve menare nelli negotiamenti della mercantia, cambii . . . opera non più veduta, composta per Aluise Casanoua . . . Venetia, 1558. Essentially one long exemplification of a set of double-entry books. Introduces several new features.

PIETRA, ANGELO: Indirizzo degli economi, o sia ordinatissima instruttione da regolatamente formare qualunque scrittura in un libro doppio; aggiuntovi l'essemplare di un libro nobile, col suo giornale, ad uso della congregation Cassinese, dell'ordine di S. Benedetto. Con due tavole, l'una de' capitoli, et l'altra delle cose piu' degne, a pieno intendimento di ciascuno. Opera nuoua . . . Composta da Don Angelo Pietra Genouese Monaco . . . In Mantova, per Francesco Osanna, 1586. Important. Double entry applied to a monastery. Financial statements used.

BIBLIOGRAPHY

GRISOGONO, SIMON: Il mercante arricchito dal perfetto quaderniere: overo, specchio lucidissimo, nel quale si scopre ogni questione, che desiderar si possa per imparare perfettamente a tenere libro doppio . . . Tratto al stil moderno Venetia da Simon Grisogono . . . In Venetia, Vecchi, 1609. Sets himself the task of bringing up to date Casanova's book.

MOSCHETTI, GIOVANNI ANTONIO: Dell'universal trattato di libro doppii, di Gio. Antonio Moschetti, libri tre. Ne' quali con regole universali, & essempi particolari ampiamente s'insegna il modo di girar in scrittura doppia qual si voglia negotio mercantile . . . in Venetia, appresso Luca Valentini, 1610. Initiates an accounting critique of practices then prevalent. The set of double-entry books closely patented on the ones of Manzoni and Casanova.

MAINARDI, MATTEO: L'economo, overo la scrittura tutelare: scrittura mercantile formalmente regolata, con le lettere de' negotij a quella correlatiue. Il cambio reale per ogni piazza giustiamente ragguagliato, con diuersi altri quesiti utili, curiosi, e necessarij alla mercatura: il tutto fatica di Matteo Mainardi. Bologna, 1632. New features in the structure of journal and ledger entries introduced. Unimportant.

FLORI, LODOVICO: Trattato del modo di tenere il libro doppio domestico, col suo esemplare composto dal padre Lodovico Flori . . . Palermo, per il Lazzari Varese, 1677. (First edition 1636.) Follows Pietra. Highest expression of early bookkeeping for precise definitions and detailed elucidation of bookkeeping principles and mechanics.

PERI, GIOVANNI DOMENICO: Il negoziante . . . Genova 1638. Bookkeeping only incidental in this treatise of commercial customs and practices.

VENTURI, BASTIANO: Scrittura conteggiante di possessioni. Urbino, 1655. Carries forward the critique of accounting and introduces a cash journal.

VENTUROLI, GIACOMO: Scorta d'economia. Bologna 1666. Unimportant. Double entry explained by dialogue.

ZAMBELLI, ANTONIO: Mercantesche dichiarazioni della scrittura doppia. Milano, 1671. Book devoted to appraising and criticizing bookkeeping practices.

PUGLIESI, ONOFRIO SBERNIA: Prattica economica numerale . . . in Palermo, nella stamperia di Angelo Felicella, 1745. (First edition, 1671.) Slavishly follows Flori's work and at times copies him outright.

CORTICELLI, LODOVICO: Mastro di casa famigliare. Bologna, 1696. Unimportant. Concerned chiefly with laborers' payroll.

DELLA GATTA, GIACOMO: Nuova pratica di arithmetica mercantile. Milano, 1744. Double entry and single entry both discussed. Work of minor importance.

PELLEGRINO, BALUGANI: Instruzione brevissima per formare con metodo qualunque scrittura in un libro doppio, coll'esemplare dello stesso libro, e suo giornale ad uso spezialmente della gioventù modenese desiderosa d'apprendere quest'arte . . . In Modena, per Bartolomeo Soliani, 1745. Pietra's work faithfully reproduced 150 years after its publication.

BREGLIA, TOMMASO DOMENICO: Trattato di scrittura doppia baronale. Napoli, 1751. Unimportant.

SCALI, PIETRO PAOLO: Trattato del modo di tenere la scrittura dei mercanti a partite doppie, cioè all'italiana e descrizione del bilancio della prima e della seconda ragione, composto da Pietro Paolo Scali . . . In Livorno, Fantechi, 1755. Unimportant. Double entry explained by questions and answers.

FORNI, GIUSEPPE: Trattato teorico-pratico della vera scrittura doppia con suo esemplare, di Giuseppe Forni . . . Pavia, Bolzani, 1790. First serious attempt to develop a theory of double entry. Elementary and faulty.

GIRAUDEAU: La banque rendue facile aux principales nations de l'Europe. 3rd ed. Lyons, Regnault, 1769. Introduces a rudimentary theory of general accounts.

DÉGRANGE, EDMOND: La tenue des livres ou nouveau traité de comptabilité générale. Paris, Hocquart, 1795. Theory of the five general accounts.

D'ANASTASIO, NICCOLÒ: La scrittura doppia ridotta a scienza. 1803. Unimportant.

DÉGRANGE, EDMOND: Supplemént à la tenue des livres rendue facile, ou nouvelle méthode pour tenir les livres en double partie . . . Paris, Hocquart, 1804. Theory of the five general accounts.

BRUNERI, FRANCESCO: Contabilità' domestica. Torino, 1816. Accounting practices of the time criticized.

ALOARDI, LUIGI: Il ragioniere ossia corso di computisteria teorico-pratico del ragioniere Luigi Aloardi. Milano, dalla tipografia di Gio. Giuseppe Destefanis, 1817. Unimportant.

BERTOLOTTI, LUIGI: L'anonimo modenese o difesa della scrittura doppia e confutazione del metodo inglese di Edoardo Tomaso Jones. Modena, 1822. Defends double entry and confutes Edward Thomas Jones' system.

WATTENHOFFER: Scienza del computista Ragionato. Modena, 1830. Unimportant.

GALLI, ANGELO: Istituzioni di contabilità, coi metodi teorico-pratici per eseguirne le operazioni. Roma, tipografia Contedini, 1837. Based on the "cinquecontisti" theory.

BORNACCINI, GIUSEPPE: Idee teoriche e pratiche di ragioneria, e di doppio giro di registrazione per le amministrazioni publiche e private e queste si civili che commerciali di Giuseppe Bornaccini di Rimini. Nuova ed. riveduta dall'autore . . . 2. ed. Rimini, tipografia Marsoner e Grandi, 1838. Unimportant.

CRIPPA, LODOVICO GIUSEPPE: La scienza dei conti. 1838. An imperfect theory of accounts.

POITRAT, VALENTIN: Tenuta dei libri autodidattica conforme alla legge (articolo 8 del codice di commercio), di Valentino Poitrat . . . Prima versione italiana . . . per cura del . . . Massimino Vissian. Milano, Stabilimento Civelli, 1844. Based on the "cinquecontisti" theory.

GITTI, VINCENZO: La scrittura doppia e le sue forme 184–? Equation of double entry developed.

VILLA, FRANCESCO: La contibilità applicata alle amministrazioni private e pubbliche, ossia elementi di scienze economico-amministrative applicati alla tenuta dei registri, ed alla compilazione e revisione dei rendiconti del ragioniere agrimensore Francesco Villa . . . Milano, Monti, 1840–41. First Italian theory to oppose the French theory of the "cinquecontisti".

DEPLANQUE, LUIGI: Trattato di contabilità commerciale in partita semplice e doppia, applicata a tutti i rami di commercio e d'industria . . . di Luigi Deplanque. Milano, tipografia Guglielmini, 1846. "Cinquecontisti" theory.

TANTINI, VINCENZO: Manuale Teorico-pratico della contabilità, comp. da Vincenzo Tantini . . . Firenze, a spese dell'autore, 1852. Based on the "cinquecontisti" theory.

VILLA, FRANCESCO: Elementi di Amministrazione e contabilità, del ragioniere-agrimensore Francesco Villa . . . 2. ed. riv. dall'autore. Pavia, Bizzoni, 1853. Second edition of the 1840 copy.

VANNIER, HIPPOLYTE: La tenue des livres telle qu'on la practique réellement dans le commerce et dans la banque; où, cours complet de comptabilité commerciale . . . par Hippolyte Vannier . . . 4. tirage. Paris, Hachette, 1854. French personalistic theory. Opposes the "cinquecontisti" theory.

BIBLIOGRAPHY

PARMETLER, FILIPPO: Elementi di computisteria e di tenuta dei libri in partita doppia ad uso dei giovani commercianti e degli alunni degli istituti technici del regno, compilati secondo il programma ufficiale, da Filippo Parmetler . . . Torino, Paravia, 1863. Propagates the French "cinquecontisti" theory.

MARCHI, FRANCESCO: I cinquecontisti. 1867. First Italian personalistic theory. Deals death blow to the "cinquecontisti" theory.

TARCHIANI, ILARIO: Guida teorica-pratica sulle scritture comparate ossia per bilancio, per Ilario Tarchiani . . . Firenze, Bencini, 1868. Modern journal described.

RIVA, MICHELE: La partita doppia e l'amministrazione dello stato, delle provincie e dei comuni. 1869. Theory of logismography.

CERBONI, GIUSEPPE: Prima saggi di logismografia all'undecimo congresso degli scienziati italiani in Roma. Roma, Botta, 1872. Theory of logismography. Personalistic theory carried to its logical conclusion.

LAPI, LUIGI: Contabilità applicata a diverse aziende, di Luigi Lapi. Siena, tip. dell'ancora di G. Bargellini, 1873. Unimportant.

GAGLIARDI, ENRICO: Saggi di computisteria e ragioneria, del . . . Enrico Gagliardi. 1. Dei conti correnti a metodo diretto italiano a forma sinottica-descrittiva. Livorno, Meucci, 1881. Unimportant.

CERBONI, GIUSEPPE: Mémoire sur l'importance d'unifier les Études de la Comptabilité: mémoire présenté au Congrès littéraire international (réuni à Rome le 20 mai 1882), par . . . Joseph Cerboni . . . Rome, Botta, 1882. Theory of Logismography.

PEZERIL, E. A.: Premiers éléments de Logismographie, par E. A. Pezeril . . . Paris, Victor Rozier, 1886. Logismography.

BESTA, FABIO: La ragioneria. 2. ed., riveduta ed ampliata col concorso dei professori Vittorio Alfieri . . . Carlo Ghidiglia . . . Pietro Rigobon . . . Milano, Vallardi, 1922–1929. Treatise on the practice, theory, and history of accounting. Value or positive theory of the account expounded. Displaced logismography.

CERBONI, GIUSEPPE: Memorandum al R. Governo e . . . sullo istituto del riscontro contabile nell'azienda dello Stato. Roma, tipografia elzeviriana, 1895. Logismography.

INDEX

INDEX

INDEX

153

INDEX

This Book was printed by The Rumford Press at Concord, New Hampshire, on paper specially made by S. D. Warren Company, and was bound by J. F. Tapley Co., of New York.

The type face is Italian Old Style, which Frederic W. Goudy designed for the Lanston Monotype Company after a study of the best early Italian faces. It suggests the distinctive Roman letter used by Erhard Ratdolt in the earliest printed works on mathematical subjects of the Renaissance Period.

The symbols used in designing the end papers and the hand-drawn initials were suggested and sketched by Mina Peloubet. The three cities in which the double-entry method first emerged, Venice, Florence, and Genoa, are represented respectively by the Lion of St. Mark, the Crowned Lily, and St. George and the Dragon. The merchant trade is symbolized by the ship under sail and the practice of book-keeping by the hourglass, quill and sandbox, and the ledger.

The book was designed by William K. Wilson, of The Rumford Press, to be in keeping with the spirit of the typography of those early Italian treatises on accounting which are known for their beauty as well as their historical interest.

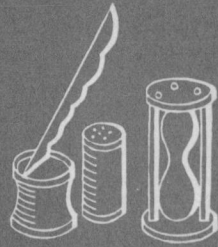

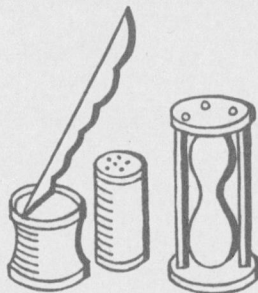